We. Me. It.

Compelling insights into the essence of human motivation

Joan-Mary Hinds PhD

First published in 2016 by Hinds Workforce Research Pty Ltd trading as Peoplepie Surveys, Australia.

Available from Amazon, Kindle and other retail outlets
Printed by CreateSpace
Cover design by Marylouise Brammer

ISBN-13:	978-0994603609 (Peoplepie Surveys)
ISBN-10:	0994603606
Author:	Joan-Mary Hinds
Title:	We. Me. It.: compelling insights into the essence of human motivation
Edition:	1st ed.
Subjects:	Management Motivation Employee Motivation

DEDICATION

Neville Albert Hinds

(1927 – 2009)

Joan-Mary Hinds PhD

Joan-Mary is a highly qualified researcher and innovator in the field of employee motivation. She has wide experience as psychologist, teacher, university lecturer, human resources director, government advisor, speaker and author. Her consultancy, Hinds Research, has assisted many government and business organisations large and small to measure and improve people motivation, performance and business outcomes.

Joan-Mary invites readers to e-mail her at joan-mary.hinds@hindsresearch.com

www.hindsresearch.com

Louisa Vanderkruk

Louisa has been a major contributor to the research and consulting activity that underpin the ideas discussed in this book. She is Founder and CEO of Peoplepie Surveys - the online platform built to deliver 'We. Me. It.' motivation tools to managers, teams and business.

www.peoplepie.com

CONTENTS

INTRODUCTION

What is motivation?

WE ALL KNOW MOTIVATION when we feel it, even if we don't quite understand it, we enjoy the sensation. We recall with pleasure our experiences of being motivated in the past, and actively seek to be motivated again. This is because motivation is both a happy and productive condition.

It's also a very complex phenomenon, but we all know from personal experience exactly what it means to us and what it can deliver. Being motivated means that we are stimulated, active, energetic, enthusiastic, happy and feeling alive. We have "get up and go", we have initiative and a sense of purpose. It also means we can achieve some amazing things.

On the other hand, not being motivated can be a problem for us. Long periods of lacking motivation are uncomfortable and can be physically painful. Periods of low or no motivation cause us concern: we worry that our natural vitality seems to have disappeared, or has been extinguished. In extreme cases unmotivated people will describe themselves as feeling uninterested, listless, dissatisfied, unresponsive, or even depressed.

As a result, there's now a whole industry of motivational speakers and gurus to deal with the problem. They can command high prices for what is mostly a temporary outcome. We feel motivated straight after hearing one of them speak, but a few days later we're back to our old selves. The motivation industry, like the slimming industry, flourishes on failure. We will line up for the next fix once the last one has come to nothing. Why is this so?

Motivation is very important to us as individuals because it means we experience an appetite for, and satisfaction in, life itself. It's also important in the people around us.

Motivated students learn more quickly, retain information for longer and gain greater pleasure in the learning. Motivated friends and relatives are more cheerful, more responsive and responsible, and provide a more open environment for play and leisure. Motivated employees work with more enthusiasm, achieve more in a shorter time, feel greater satisfaction and remain loyal to their jobs and organisations.

A little scientific terminology might be helpful here. Motivation is the experience or condition that accompanies the flow of positive energy found in humans. The energy source is based on what is variously known as instincts, needs or drives – a reminder of humans' membership of the animal kingdom. Survival is an example of an instinct, need or drive. These needs – I'll use this word throughout the book for simplicity sake – are usually expressed to achieve an objective, or some type of fulfilment. When they're being expressed or used, the individual is feeling or being motivated.

By contrast, needs can be blocked or prevented from being expressed: this is *negative motivation*, the opposite of motivation. To illustrate the difference, imagine a tiger. In the wild where the tiger is mating and hunting, it is expressing its needs. Once a tiger is confined to a cage, the tiger's needs are being blocked and repressed.

This example of energy in the wild versus confinement in the cage underpins the theme of this book. It provides a visual example of the expression and suppression of needs in the wider family of animals to which humans belong. In humans, as in other animals, needs can be *expressed* or *suppressed.* Understanding this – expression versus suppression – is a key to understanding motivation.

My motivated career

Before we go any further I should share a little about my personal journey, which is really what's behind this book.

I've spent over four decades researching, investigating and working in the field of workplace motivation and dynamics. With a foundation in social work, clinical and depth psychology, secondary and tertiary education, arts administration, government policy development and human resources management, my path finally led to the establishment of a successful research consultancy, whose clients have provided much of the rich material for understanding human motivation and its dynamics at work.

Milestones along my journey have included:

- Early clinical and academic focus on understanding boredom (and thus motivation), particularly in students and employees
- Original research to identify the preconditions (causes) of employee motivation beyond simple external stimulation
- Further original research to develop the Hinds Motivation–Boredom Continuum
- Construction of the Tripartite Motivation Model
- Creation of an award-winning employee motivation survey
- Delivery of people-performance enhancing research and action solutions for many clients.

Along the way I've been awarded a number of degrees: BA (1961) from the University of Western Australia, MA (1982) and MA Hons (1988) in Education from Macquarie University in Sydney, and finally a PhD (1993) in Management from Macquarie Graduate School of Management.

In 1995, my insights and the results of my investigations were published in Australia in *The Hinds Model of Company Success* (Millennium Press). What you're now reading represents an update on that earlier work, and is expanded to include subsequent findings and theoretical development.

To support my work, I've had scholarly articles accepted in the publications of bodies such as Australian and New Zealand Academy of Management (ANZAM) New Directions in Management, International Decision Sciences Institute, World Innovation and Strategy Symposium, and Australian Centre for Research in Employment and Work. I've also presented more than 80 papers and scholarly talks to professional and academic bodies.

The employee motivation survey developed from my research and consulting work won a number of professional awards for innovation and change, including the 1992 ANZAM award for research excellence. It was then made available for commercial use under the name the Employee Motivation and Performance Index (EMPI®). This instrument has been further improved and has been adapted specifically for teams and smaller business groups. It is now available for managers and business to use through Peoplepie. (www.peoplepie.com)

EMPI® was been widely used in the private and government sectors via Hinds Workforce Research, the research consultancy I established in 1989. The consultancy continues today as Hinds Research and strives to improve employee motivation and performance through the application of research to support evidence-based change, leadership and management practices. It now has a special focus on teachers and students in terms of motivation in education.

Over the past 25 years, the consultancy team has conducted tailored culture projects for more than 100 medium to large private and public sector organisations (i.e. Australian Bureau of Statistics, AXA, Brambles, Centrelink, New Zealand Post, Australian Federal Police and Westpac to name just a few). We have surveyed more than 227,000 employees in 13 languages in more than 40 countries. Our extensive data has validated, confirmed and refined the theories and models of human and employee motivation that are found in this book.

My findings in a nutshell...

The main findings you'll read in this book are simple and straightforward.

- Current business management and organisational psychology thinking suggests widespread acceptance of a needs-based theoretical approach to understanding and defining employee motivation

- This book belongs firmly in the 'needs-based motivation' school of thought

- The origin of human motivation is derived from the operation of three intrinsic needs (instincts or drives), an echo of our animal instincts for procreation and survival, with the addition of an exclusively human dimension – the need for spirituality or creativity

- Higher levels of motivation occur as a result of the expression or satisfaction of these three human needs. In the workplace, these can be understood as the need for:
    - Affiliation (bonding, friendship or community)
    - Achievement (winning, success or recognition)
    - Actualisation (meaning, vocation or creativity)

- Motivation operates on a continuum with its opposite commonly known as boredom. Positive aspects of employee motivation are matched by their negatives, or types of boredom. Thus we have the

Affiliation need on a continuum from interest to apathy, the Achievement need running from satisfaction to frustration, and the Actualisation need running from commitment to escapism

- The behaviours and sensations along the length of the positive/negative continuum provide a set of symptoms that accurately measure the levels of motivation to de-motivation or boredom

- The three needs (Affiliation, Achievement, and Actualisation) that underpin motivation are universal, but vary in dominance from one individual to the next depending upon their personality, life stage and circumstances. For motivation to exist, all three needs must be expressed or satisfied, even if to varying degrees at different times

- The key precondition or cause of human motivation is achieving the correct balance between freedom and order or structure
- Extensive empirical research has defined and solidified this precondition by identifying seven main factors that significantly impact on, or operate as drivers for employee motivation: these are Job, Alignment, Employer, Development, Influence, Manager and Leadership

- Each of the seven drivers contains a set of workplace features that provide a balance between freedom and structure

- Effecting or raising employee motivation delivers a positive knock-on effect to organisational performance, which in turn leads to a reduction of business problems and an increase in employee loyalty, sales, business success and ultimately profits.

Why should we care about motivation?

Human motivation is a fascinating topic, and understanding motivation and its dynamics carries implications for all of us in our personal and professional lives. Many people tell me how much they would like to understand what motivates their families, their friends, their employees, and their colleagues. Every detective or 'whodunnit' story is underpinned by the search for motivation: to find out why, who benefits, and to track the perpetrator. The springs of human motivation form the bedrock of all the creative arts, and explain history and indeed all human events including war and peace.

An understanding of motivation provides us with greater emotional intelligence and capacity for more successful management of both our work and play. It provides a better foundation from which to conduct our affairs, whether private or on the world stage. It provides an opportunity for leaders in any situation to set the path, inspire the loyalty, set the measures and implement the actions for higher employee motivation and higher productivity.

This book will help you to unravel the mysteries behind human and specifically employee motivation. It doesn't offer easy tricks or sure-fire methods. It does however; provide easy access to understanding our own motivations, and thereby to explore how these operate in the workplace. My work on motivation was directed initially to students and education and was later extended to include management and organisations. But such knowledge will assist anyone who deals with or helps people, such as teachers, nurses, politicians, community workers and of course parents.

Motivation is the energy force that separates the exciting from the mundane. It's the source of vitality and capacity to derive satisfaction and enjoyment from life and work. Consciously or unwittingly, everyone is interested in motivation, or at least in being motivated, and that's the best reason to read on.

CHAPTER 1: FROM DARKNESS INTO LIGHT

A new path to an old problem

I WAS A SECONDARY SCHOOL TEACHER for a decade between 1964 and 1974 and like most teachers, I wanted to motivate my students and keep them motivated. I knew that a motivated student is easier to teach, more attentive, produces better work, learns more quickly, is more imaginative and creative, and will ultimately achieve higher grades. I wasn't lacking for guidance: many academic, anecdotal and research offerings had advice on the best ways to motivate students.

The funny thing was that I had never heard my students talk about motivation; instead they often complained of "being bored". So it occurred to me that looking for the secret to motivate students might be setting the cart before the horse.

In casual conversation, my friends would complain of being bored when they were at school and how it turned them away from further education and opportunities in life. "I couldn't wait to leave school," they'd tell me. "It was so boring." They remembered boring teachers with great bitterness; they dropped out of courses just to avoid boring subject matter.

Plenty of educational commentators agreed. In 1969, the famous English writer, teacher and broadcaster Edward Blishen wrote: "Students say that school is boring – it is a word that unites all the essays that allow themselves to be freely critical." Blishen sought comments from his students. Robin, aged 13, said: "What a bore school is nowadays, the same as it has been for 100 years." Carol, 16, claimed: "Lessons should not be a drag like the boring English teacher." "Maths is so boring…." said Ursula, 15.

In 1970, the USA's Assistant Commissioner of Elementary and Secondary Education, Leon Lessinger, said: "Many students, when asked what their dominant feeling in school is, answer with the single word 'boredom'."

But of what were these students complaining? And how could teachers and educators avoid "boring" their charges and being responsible for such widespread boredom?

Thus began my rather unusual interest in, and study of, student boredom in secondary schools and tertiary institutions. I noted that boredom was a besetting problem and a major barrier to scholastic and academic achievement. I argued that in approaching the issue of student motivation, surely one first needed to understand the problem of student de-motivation and boredom.

On the dark side of the moon

Whilst student motivation was, and continues to be, a topic of educational concern, little attention was being paid to boredom. I undertook a literature review in 1981, which demonstrated that boredom had been a neglected topic and was, as a result, wide open for further academic investigation. Bearing in mind the limited means of access in a pre-digital world, at that time only 15 papers on boredom in school or elsewhere had been published. Boredom appeared to be somewhat of a mystery in all branches of psychology. Motivation was widely explored, but boredom as a topic had been academically neglected. It was the dark side of the moon, where the light of knowledge had not penetrated.

Even now, boredom is rarely linked with motivation. Rather, it's viewed as either an interesting subject for philosophy and literature. There are now two mainstream examples of this approach: The Demon of Noontide: Ennui in Western Literature by Reinhard Kuhn (1976), tracing the condition and its names from antiquity to the present day, and more recently Boredom: The Literary History of a State of Mind by Patricia Meyer Spacks (1995), tracing its shifting cultural uses.

Alternatively, boredom is regarded as a serious clinical condition or pathology by therapists such as Otto Fenichel (1951) and his "pathological boredom as a defense mechanism of repression", or as character trait by psychologists such as Amos Drury (1982) and his "boredom proneness personality". However, because it has not been widely studied, even today the number of references and investigations into boredom as a permanent or transient condition are strictly limited. The workplace researcher Cynthia Fisher maintained in 1993 that it is a "neglected concept" and in a review of studies from 1926 to 1981, by the American authority Richard P Smith (1981) commented that "articles concerning boredom averaged less than one paper a year".

Later in this book, we will touch on how far this neglect of the topic of boredom and its isolation or division from the topic of motivation persists, even to the present day. But to make sense of emerging concepts in more current studies, we need to continue on our own path into an understanding of the nature and dynamics of boredom.

In everyday discourse our conversation flows easily from boredom to motivation and back; but in the disciplines of literary or historical analysis, psychology, education, business and others, the two conditions have usually been approached and understood as separate and different.

Journeying to the dark side

Thus I began my journey to the dark side of the moon: to the world of boredom, the very antithesis of motivation.

First I wanted to find out why boredom had been a neglected topic. A clue came from everyday experience. When asked about the topic, colleagues and friends rejected it as frivolous. Most adults denied ever being bored. Some became defensive or even angry when asked about their experience of boredom, as if it were a fault of individual character. "I'm too busy to ever be bored," they said. Or they might say; "If you're bored you have too much time on your hands."

Among managers there was a similar response of blame or shame. When asked about bored employees, a computer company executive responded: "You won't find anyone bored here because we just sack them." Another executive told me: "In my position, I don't have the luxury of being bored."

Beyond blame and shame, boredom is an unpleasant subject because it's linked to so many very unpleasant, even painful, sensations, feelings and behaviours; to say the least, it's an uncomfortable condition to think about.

A short history of boredom

Society is now one polish'd horde,
Form'd of two mighty tribes, the Bores and Bored
(Lord Byron, Don Juan, 1823)

The word "boredom" is often attributed first to Charles Dickens, because it appears six times in his novel Bleak House, published in 1852–53. Whilst most dictionaries follow Dickens' definition in suggesting that boredom is a muted sensation of weariness or dullness, its etymological origins link it to the much earlier and more aggressive Old English "borian", meaning to "plough or pierce or hollow into".

Although most authorities dismiss this earlier link, I urge you to accept it. This sense of being attacked is important to understanding why boredom is often so psychologically unpleasant. In 1622, the eminent Jacobean English playwright John Fletcher wrote: "I am laughed at, scorned, baffled and bored it seems by my English friends." By 1768, the word boredom continued to have a sense of being irritated according to the Earl of Carlisle: "I have pity for my Newmarket friends who are to be bored by these Frenchmen." It wasn't until later with the writings of Dickens, that the meaning of the word and indeed the condition of boredom moved to mean some sort of lassitude – as expressed in Dickens' published attack on the proposed legislation to restrict recreational activity for workers on Sundays. "You offer no relief from listlessness... he saunters moodily around weary and dejected...in lieu of the wholesome stimulus to be derived from nature ..." Here, Dickens combines the widely-accepted modern take on the nature and causes of boredom.

However, boredom is not the most widely used word for this human malaise. Looking to the classics, we find boredom in all its complexity appearing in Western literature throughout historical times under a range of different names.

In ancient Greek texts boredom was called the dread, the malady or black gall. In early Christian texts it was acedia, or the demon of noontide. The Elizabethans knew it as the disposed monarch, ennui or melancholy. In the Enlightenment it was called spleen, nothingness or the void, and later descriptions included self-created prison, sterility, indifference, life-in-death, spiritual lassitude and surrealist sorrow. Boredom is, if nothing else, well known and well documented in human history, culture and art.

The more I researched, the more it became clear that boredom is indeed a highly complex condition with a range of rather nasty negative emotions, behaviours and sensations.

According to the literature, boredom can include a myriad of unpleasant emotions and sensations: a sense of servitude, monotony, repetition, sense of routine, of dullness, lack of interest, lack of control, immobility, forced passivity, enforced silence, and lack of support.

Behaviours associated with boredom are just as diverse. Bored people may exhibit deterioration of performance, mental skills and attention or loss of intellectual capacity and control. They can be over-sensitive and behave childishly. They might lose their sense of constraint. Fatigue is common. The list of behaviours includes loss of satisfaction, pleasure or interest; depression or misery; sadness, non-specific tension; restlessness, aggression, hostility, anxiety, loss of confidence… and more.

The unpleasant sensations and behaviours associated with boredom probably explain why some colleagues with whom I spoke rejected the idea of ever being bored. It may also explain the neglect of the topic in the scientific and psychological literature - beyond its pathological manifestations.

Is monotony the cause of boredom?

So what makes people bored? Where it has been studied, the main assumption was (and to a great extent is still today) that boredom is caused by repetition or lack of stimulation. The landmark investigation 'Effects of decreased variation in the sensory environment' (by McGill University medical researchers W.H. Bexton, W. Heron and T.H. Scott in 1954) looked into the impacts of prolonged isolation and severe lack of stimulation. It confirmed that they cause boredom and that it is indeed a psychologically uncomfortable condition, and that it can also be physically painful.

A side consideration offered by this extraordinary laboratory experiment is its demonstration that boredom proceeds through a series of increasingly unpleasant stages, the longer it is endured. According to the authors' observations, the subjects moved from the less severe condition of sadness and sleepiness to a more severe anger, depression and restlessness and finally to a psychically and even physically painful stage of confusion, headaches and hallucinations. Boredom's capacity to pass through various stages of increasing intensity or severity the longer it continues became an important feature in my understanding of the nature of boredom. I'll consider this further in later chapters.

But let's for the moment continue to focus on the causes of boredom. Those found in the field of educational psychology were of particular interest to me. In 1968, the educator John Paul De Cecco wrote:

"Boredom arises from a monotonous environment or the performance of repetitive tasks. Boredom, also called stimulus deprivation or isolation, leads to inattention."

Reviewing further material from school classroom observations, I noted that monotony or lack of stimulation was widely accepted as the culprit for boredom in the educational setting. For example, in 1964, the French language teacher Chester W. Obuchowski provided a compelling set of observations about the "breeders of ennui" in school and notes his observations about "the unremitting repetition… the dullest of dull classes… the sameness of things gives birth to boredom… a pall of grey monotony descends upon the classroom".

So, in the early 1980s when my own investigations began, the accepted wisdom about the cause of student boredom was insufficient variety, inadequate stimulation and monotony. Similar assumptions applied to the world of work. I recall a friend, the owner/manager of a food processing plant, asserting that employee boredom was unavoidable – indeed, it was inevitable if one was engaged in slicing jam rolls all day. "Some jobs are just plain repetitive, monotonous and boring," he said.

Most authorities simply stated, in different ways, the tautology that "boredom is caused by boring lessons or work". The matter appeared to be closed.

I chose to keep it open. There was more to learn.

My eureka moment

As a Sydney University Teachers College lecturer, in 1985, I attended a presentation by a visiting American educator on the topic of teacher-promoted student imagination. Sitting in the audience, highly motivated and focused, I found to my amazement that I switched off; so much so that I missed a full five minutes of the talk. I'd apparently become bored and inattentive. This was very irritating because there was no way to recover the information I'd missed.

Travelling home in my car, I thought about what had happened. The experience of "switching off" was puzzling, particularly as I'd been so interested in the presentation topic, and highly motivated to attend. My reaction during the lecture troubled me more than the loss of information. I knew from my readings of research papers that student interest and stimulation underpinned motivation. However, here was an instance of being in a state of high interest and high stimulation yet slipping easily into boredom. I'd been so bored that my mind wandered completely, that I had, in the colloquial phrase, "blanked out".

Once at home, I looked at the notes I'd made during the lecture and found the exact moment when boredom had intervened. The visiting educator had offered an opinion with which I completely disagreed. Constrained by courtesy and the very public situation, I'd had to swallow my disagreement and stay silent. Voila! I'd switched off and experienced boredom for some minutes. My high motivation to listen had been undermined, not by monotony, lack of stimulation or by repetition, but by the suppression of a strongly held opinion.

All the authorities that I'd read to that point had offered lack of stimulation, repetition or monotony as the cause of boredom. Here, I'd run into a new insight. The cause of my boredom in this case wasn't simply lack of stimulation, but lack of an opportunity to express a strongly held opinion or idea. I was unable to speak up and speak out. This was my Eureka moment.

As with all new insights, this didn't come as a complete surprise. Steeped as I was in Freudian psychology, I'd long ago accepted that negative sensations are associated with the blocking or suppression of innate needs or instincts. As a trigger for boredom, suppressing the desire to speak or question was certainly new, but consistent with my academic tradition.

I'd uncovered what appeared to be a second cause of boredom. Reflecting on my own experiences, I realised that freedom to speak out or argue had been a common characteristic of the livelier classrooms and lecture halls I'd known. It underlined my observations that students allowed to verbalise opinions and express themselves seemed less prone to boredom.

Education authorities, as far as I could see, agreed that boredom in students led to educational failure. But there were only hints that, beyond monotony, another cause of student boredom might be the suppression of speaking up, the denial of open verbalisation. Students themselves provide more definite and clearer support for this second cause. In 1983, teacher John Marsh recorded comments by his students about boredom in class. "I wanted to be belligerent, but I was too choked off…I just stifled my comments" offered one student. "If I do say something it will probably come out wrong…So I'm sitting back and not saying anything," offered another.

I decided to demonstrate scientifically that suppression of verbalisation was a significant cause of boredom. Thus I set about conducting multiple qualitative and quantitative investigations with students from three different schools (for a full description of this research see the Sidebar "The war between the planets"). In short, the results of this investigation demonstrated that boredom is not simply caused by repetition and lack of stimulation, but more often by constraints on student verbal expression, especially of student negation. By this I mean that the student goes beyond offering a comment or an opinion but takes a negative stance such as "I don't agree", "I think you are wrong", "I don't understand what you mean" or "I think it should be different". Even a sincere information-seeking question from a student can be interpreted by a teacher as negation, as it may seem to call into question their statements or authority.

Teacher responses to student comments, questions or negation are all too often suppressors of motivation. They might be brushed to one side ("not now, later"), dismissed ("that's not relevant here"), belittled ("that's a silly question") or seen as a correction ("don't be impudent") or even as an attack ("it's rude to interrupt"). As a practicing teacher I have sympathy with this negative reaction to student verbalization, given the pressure of the classroom and its curriculum objectives. However, a question or comment delayed is more serious than failing to cover the subject material – losing student involvement, interest and attention is far more serious. My surveys confirmed that students got bored when they were unable to speak up, speak out, disagree or generally express themselves.

The motivation–boredom continuum

I'd reached a stage of understanding that boredom was a consequence of the denial of freedom to offer an opinion, comment, question or negation. However, almost as important as the discovery of 'suppression of verbalisation' as a cause of boredom was the fact that motivation could turn directly and seamlessly into boredom. Here was a continuum!

This new insight held important implications for my investigations. I realised that boredom and motivation operate as opposite sides of the same coin – that boredom is the reverse of motivation. And that boredom and motivation are linked by a common chain moving from positive to negative.

As my research continued, it became obvious that I was, unexpectedly, approaching the popular topic of motivation by means of examining boredom. The study of boredom is the study of motivation – only in reverse. The extreme negative of high levels of boredom exists on a continuum with high levels of motivation as the extreme positive. Low levels of both boredom and motivation fall somewhere in the middle.

Figure: The Motivation-Boredom Continuum

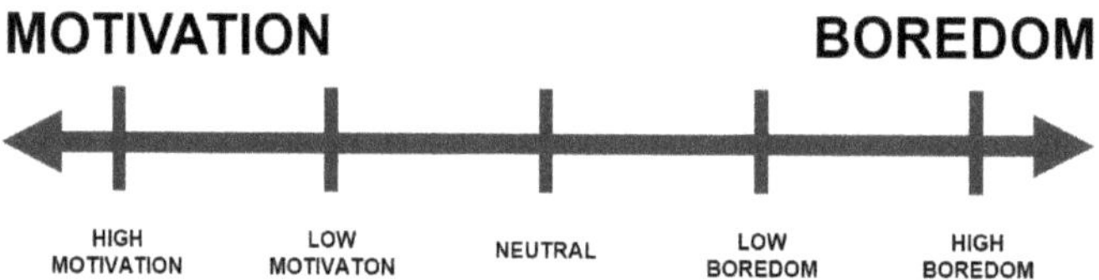

By now my academic career was moving from the field of education into the field of business management and organizational development. My professional life had moved from teaching and psychology into human resources and organizational development. At the same time, there was a growing commercial and academic interest in the understanding and measurement of employee motivation (or its preferred emerging term, employee engagement).

I was probably one of the first to recognise that, if one was to accurately measure employee motivation, the survey ought to include questions about boredom, motivation's negative. A measure that ended with low motivation or low engagement and didn't extend to include levels of boredom would in fact be missing half the picture. Think of it this way: measuring motivation without including the negative dimension of boredom is like measuring company profits in terms of revenues without including costs and debt. The opposite of motivation is not low motivation; it's boredom!

Low motivation or low boredom are mid points between two extremes – the equivalent, in financial terms, of low profit and low debt. I discovered that most previous measures of employee motivation simply started at high motivation and stopped at low motivation, but failed to reach down to the depths of boredom: either low or severe boredom.

As a consequence of experiencing the movement between the two conditions, I immediately shifted the focus of my PhD research in Business Management to explore both boredom and motivation. I decided to test empirically my hypotheses that a) the two states of motivation and boredom exist on a continuum and that b) boredom is caused, not simply by lack of stimulation but also, by the suppression of verbalisation. In reverse, motivation is caused or promoted by the freedom to express ideas, comments, questions or negation. In other words, both states respond to the expression (in the case of motivation) or suppression (boredom) of human needs.

Fortunately, at that point in time, my "day job" was working as a human resources director at Capita, an Australian insurance and investment company; now no longer operating, but then employing more than 1500 people. So I had in front of me a perfect research population upon which to test my theories on boredom, motivation and their dynamics in the workplace.

A medical investigation model

Knowing that boredom was the opposite of motivation was a vital clue in developing a useful and more scientific set of motivation measures. Up until then, researchers had used only positive symptoms of motivation such as satisfaction, interest and engagement. By contrast, I was able to include the negative symptoms of boredom such as apathy, frustration and escapism.

This replicated the diagnostic approach of medical doctors, who don't ask patients about their symptoms of health, but about symptoms of their illness or sickness. By also investigating the symptoms of boredom, I'd get a much more accurate reading of motivation, and my search for the causes would also be more reliable. Rather than simply studying the "healthy" state and causes of motivation, I would concurrently be investigating the unhealthy state, or "sickness", of boredom or apathy.

My PhD research would use a large quantitative survey administered to all of Capita's employees. My research topics for exploration were:

- Motivation
- Boredom, and
- Workplace preconditions that might influence both motivation and boredom – including external monotony and suppression of verbalisation

I wanted to know how motivation and boredom operated in employees and also what workplace factors made a difference, either positive or negative. The challenge was to identify the organisational programs, management styles, human resources practices, work culture and leadership characteristics that have the greatest impact on employee motivation.

My approach to understanding motivation through the negative dimension of boredom had some advantages. Primarily because boredom is an uncomfortable, even painful experience its symptoms, emotions, behaviours or signals are much more noticeable than the gentler and more diffuse experiences of motivation and happiness. Individuals are able to know when they are bored more readily and more confidently. They know when they are sleepy, irritated, frustrated, restless or seeking escape because these conditions cause psychic, even physical, discomfort or pain. So respondents answering a survey on employee motivation can be more certain of their answers when some of the questions are about boredom.

With my aims and method clear, I crafted the survey, which was completed by the employees of Capita.

The results of the investigation were as I'd hoped. They demonstrated that the opposite of motivation was not just low motivation, but was indeed boredom. The survey also identified the most potent drivers of employee motivation in the workplace and hence the most potent drivers of boredom. And finally, it brought forward a new and interesting insight into the nature of motivation, from which I began constructing a new model of employee motivation.

Unleashing the giant

In the dear old analog days of 1989, it was no mean feat to convince the management team of the financial services company Capita to allow me to go ahead with my PhD survey. At the time, most organisation leaders were only just becoming comfortable with the use of employee opinion surveys, and a 30 per cent response rate was considered more than adequate. After all, who really cared about the silent majority? However, the investigation I'd planned wasn't merely an information-gathering exercise. It was hypothesis-testing research, and it had to meet the higher standards required for academic rigour. Scientific accuracy demanded a questionnaire exploring a very wide range of variables and a response rate of at least 85 per cent to remove statistical error or bias.

The company had just over 1,500 employees working in a wide range of occupations from professional, administration, service and sales, to geriatric careers and unskilled labourers. Alongside information collected from academic and professional literature, I gathered qualitative information from focus groups to inform the content, nature and wording of the survey. The 15 employee discussion groups were made up of randomly selected executives and employees representative of a range of demographic characteristics.

The survey was necessarily extensive – it had to cover a lot of ground and endeavor to provide answers to many queries. Is motivation linked to boredom and how? Which are the most potent drivers of motivation or boredom in the workplace? Was it possible to identify significant differences between employees, so that they could be allocated to distinct segments in their response to, or experience of, motivation?

The survey topics covered both cause and effect of employee motivation and boredom. First, it included all the possible antecedents, causes or drivers of both motivation and boredom (including work, company, management, colleagues, environment, power, service, image, rewards, communication, change, reviews, career, training and personal issues). Second, it included all the symptoms (sensations and behaviours) of both motivation and boredom, bearing in mind that at this stage the condition and drivers of motivation were offered as different from the condition and drivers of boredom.

I made the survey easier to complete by using a short form of a Likert response scale, which requires responses to statements (not questions) on a five-point agreement/disagreement scale. I used colloquial language and humour lifted from the focus groups to make completing the document a more pleasurable experience. However it was still a huge task for respondents. The final survey questionnaire included a whopping 522 items; to which were added demographic questions to identify employee features such as status, age, gender, role and more.

Today, such an exercise would not be acceptable. Surveys are far too common and frequent and no company would tolerate a questionnaire of such length and complexity. However, at the time, this was an innovative event and was planned accordingly. As the initiating and responsible human resources manager in charge of the project – and indeed protected by CEO sponsorship – I was able to get away with murder!

The high completion and response rate for the hard-copy questionnaire was achieved due to five key tactics:

1. Repeated communication at all levels directed to individuals

2. Branding and a catchy title – "Have your say on survey day" – which encouraged employees to see it as an opportunity, not an imposition

3. Standardised unvarying structure of questions in statement format with simple response rating for ease of completion

4. Simple, colloquial language enlivened with humour and fun

5. Survey completion using a census-style, classroom format, falling on one day across the whole organisation

The survey took each employee about 40 minutes to complete. With the good fortune of a supportive CEO and the necessary budget, and to the amazement and pleasure of company leadership, the survey achieved an impressive 89% response rate, which delivered valid and reliable results. This was an extraordinary outcome for 1989. Today, obtaining high response rates is much easier because surveys are completed online, employees are familiar with the process, which occurs regularly, and they receive many electronic prompts to take part.

My survey data provided a solid foundation for statistical analysis that in turn yielded compelling insights and information about employees, their motivation, and complex workplace dynamics. Sadly Capita was by then failing (due to a combination of de-mutualisation and expensive expansion) and had become a takeover target. So we had only a few months to benefit from the knowledge before new brooms started the redundancy processes and turned off the lights.

However, what little was done was impressive. First we found that some of the employees with the lowest survey scores were also the newest, and Human Resources was able to pick up a serious selection issue. It turned out new employees were being employed on the basis of the selecting manager's own preferences – for instance, because a candidate had attended a private school, or lived in an 'elite' suburb, or dare we say, was well dressed. Once we discovered that this type of applicant was frequently very low on motivation and a poor performer, the selection criteria was changed.

A senior sales manager responsible for 20 sales teams instigated a second change. Together he and I reviewed team motivation scores against sales performance indicators, and found that low motivation predicted lower sales performance. He was amazed to learn that this was the case 100% of the time. He wanted to fix this. So we were able to introduce a team development program to encourage the company sales force to verbalise and participate more openly in their regular meetings.

For my PhD, the data supported my speculations around the link between motivation and boredom, and the importance of suppression of verbalisation as a cause of boredom in addition to the previously favoured monotony or lack of stimulation. The investigation also confirmed that symptoms of motivation clustered with symptoms of boredom, and that motivation is the opposite of, and exists on a continuum with, boredom.

I used separate statistical analyses of the responses to separate the symptoms of boredom and the drivers of boredom. These yielded two key conclusions. First, they showed that the symptoms of motivation measure the same thing as the symptoms of boredom, confirming my theory that motivation and boredom operate on a continuum. Second, the statistical analysis of the driver responses selected those with the highest correlation against motivation/boredom symptoms and clustered them to deliver the strongest workplace drivers of motivation.

In the years to come, I would refine my survey methods and gather data from over 200,000 employees of many different organisations. The accumulating information confirmed, modified and augmented these early findings. What was most important is that I had successfully developed a very robust measure of motivation because I had included its dimensions of boredom. I had developed a sound set of measures based on the symptoms (feelings and behaviours) of motivation/boredom and did not have to resort to fallible direct questions. Because the measure of motivation is so robust, the identification of the drivers is also probably more robust than many others available.

What did it all mean?

My PhD investigation and associated survey investigation of Capita employees had been used to demonstrate that suppression of verbalisation was also a cause of boredom, along with the widely accepted lack of stimulation and monotony.

It also sought to demonstrate that boredom is the dark side of the moon of motivation, that motivation and boredom share a continuum and can be measured by the same symptoms. For example, the frustration of boredom is simply the opposite of the positive sense of satisfaction. Frustration measures the lowest level that motivation can reach, and satisfaction the highest.

In my speculations about boredom, I'd assumed that its symptoms represented the blocking of two human needs, namely the sexual/bonding need and the aggressive/survival need, as identified by Sigmund Freud (see the beginning of the next chapter). Freud posited that humans have two main instincts; these are the need for procreation and the need for survival. Considering its application to the workplace, I had renamed the sexual need as the Affiliate need or drive and the aggressive/survival need as the Achievement need or drive.

While I waited for the statistical analysis of responses to the survey to be completed, I naturally expected to hear that the symptoms of motivation/boredom would fall into two groups, in line with Freud's hypothesis of two needs or instincts. I was in for a surprise.

When he'd completed his work on the survey, my long-term colleague, statistician and friend, Ron phoned me. "I've found three not two clusters for the symptoms of motivation/boredom," he said. "I hope you can explain this?"

What excitement. After some consideration, I replied: "Yes, I can!"

CHAPTER 2: THE SECRETS OF MOTIVATION

With a little help from Dr. Freud

BEFORE WE GO ANY FURTHER, I think it would be useful to review the foundations of my ideas, and to take a look at their primary influences.

After carefully examining the work of leading cognitive, developmental and behaviorist psychologists, I was most persuaded by the conclusions and ideas of the *needs theorists.* Their position is that human behaviors are motivated by the desire to fulfill human instincts or needs. In other words, that human motivation has intrinsic (or internal) sources. Our feelings, actions and beliefs are the result of internal needs or "innate instincts", rather than being purely extrinsic or originating externally (i.e. stimulated or coming from outside).

Some of the better-known needs theorists include, in chronological order, Sigmund Freud, Abraham Maslow, Frederick Herzberg, David McClelland, Clayton P. Alderfer, Paul Lawrence, Nitin Nohria, and Daniel Pink: (for readers interested, their various ideas are briefly considered in a later chapter).

Perhaps the most academically rigorous and more noteworthy authority, who has spawned significant research support, is Edward L. Deci, professor at the University of Rochester, New York, USA. He sets out his self-determination theory (SDT) concerning the operation of intrinsic motivation. I have a particular affection for Deci (1995). He offers a theory of motivation which is consistent with my thinking and he describes his observations and understanding in accessible language and stories. Happily for me, he also helped explain confusing and somewhat distressing opposition I encountered during my postgraduate studies at university (see "The war between the planets").

Due to my extensive training in psychoanalysis, I was primarily influenced by the theories of Sigmund Freud (1856–1939), who suggested that human motivation is derived from the two basic instincts or needs that are shared and aligned with our animal nature. These he identified as, first, the need for procreation (or the sexual drive), and second, the stronger need for survival (or the aggressive drive). According to Freud, these underpin the human experiences of sex and aggression (or love and war). He maintained that these basic animal instincts are modified in humans by the civilising influences of education and culture. He claimed that the highest human creative achievements are an expression not of a single need or instinct but of a combination and modification, melding, or synthesis, of the aggressive and sexual instincts.

The war between the planets

In his seminal 1995 book '*Why we do what we do*', Edward L. Deci suggested that "psychology has a history that is a bit like a patient with a split personality": it has two dramatically different identities. One emerged as the study of internal processes that are difficult to observe directly; namely the psychoanalytic tradition that began with Sigmund Freud's revolutionary work (*The ego and the* id, 1923). The second emerged with a single-minded focus on distinct, observable behaviours and their reinforcements; namely the empirical behaviorists and cognitive theorists, most notably offered by the Harvard professor B.F. Skinner (1974).

Sadly, Deci published this assertion – thereby offering me what would have been confidence-boosting support – after I'd finished my studies. Back in 1981, while working towards my Masters in Educational Development Psychology, I'd offered the hypothesis that encouraging students to express negative opinions would alleviate boredom and promote motivation, interest and involvement. My evidence was drawn from Freudian psychological clinical evidence and from my own personal observations. The faculty to whom I'd proposed this idea, Macquarie University's Department of Educational Psychology, which was then filled with behaviorist psychologists, was not happy. They clearly hoped that my interest in intrinsic motivation and boredom would go away – and me with it.

I stayed, and began to investigate independently the literature and evidence about student boredom in schools, and to test a new model of boredom where the causes included the suppression of intrinsic needs, specifically the need for disagreement. I was an accepted MA (Hons) student but could find no one to supervise me: apparently my hypothesis was based on academic heresy – Freudian as opposed to Skinnerian psychology. From 1980 until 1986, I went from lecturer to lecturer in the department seeking a supervisor. Eventually, time ran out on them; according to the university regulations, a supervisor had to be allocated by the department within seven years of my being accepted as a Masters student.

I well remember the committee interview in which faculty members discussed the problem – who would supervise this heretic? Finally, one bold lecturer stepped up to the plate and accepted, to my (and indeed everyone's) relief. They shook him by the hand and thanked him warmly. There were no handshakes for me! My new supervisor warned me that as a dedicated behaviorist, he would be diligent in ensuring the veracity of my empirical evidence. He didn't agree with my hypothesis and expected that it would be disproved. Nevertheless, I have every reason to be most grateful for his support, despite and perhaps especially because of his skepticism.

For this MA (Hons) project, I developed and conducted a 75-item survey that tested for 25 symptoms of boredom and a full range of possible causes, covering both monotony and constraints on freedom of expression. I used 780 secondary school students representing all four performance quartiles with roughly 50% each boys and girls and attending both state and independent schools in Sydney, Australia. The responses were collated and statistically analysed to identify factor groups and correlations. Then I waited for my supervisor to let me know the results of the analysis (in those days we did not have the software to do our own) and his comments.

He phoned late at night in a state of heightened emotion. He was amazed: "You were right – you've demonstrated your hypothesis. I can hardly believe it!" For me it simply meant that one could empirically prove the insights available from my observations and from the wisdom to be found in the Freudian branch of psychology.

My challenge was to continue to develop empirical evidence to test the insights gained from my endeavors in the field of intrinsic and needs based motivational psychology. Worn out by the behaviorist slant of Macquarie's Education Department, I transferred to the more compatible field of business and completed my PhD "Employee boredom in the workplace" in 1993 with Macquarie's Graduate School of Management: hence my move into the corporate world, and subsequent focus on employee motivation. Since then, as a paid consultant, I've been able to access separate employee populations of as large as 45,000 employees while working on various projects, which have allowed me to continue my empirical investigations and to replicate and confirm my model of employee motivation.

The fields of business and industry have made huge advances in the understanding of employee motivation, with major consultancies and universities providing extensive evidence over two decades about the drivers, dynamics and outcomes of high levels of employee motivation. The recent McCloud report from the UK led to government policy of fostering employee engagement such that "Company and organizational profitability and performance has been transformed" (Zinger 2009). My move to the world of business reflects its welcoming environment and intense interest. By contrast, in the world of education, the challenge of teacher motivation remains relatively untouched, so much so that UNESCO (2014) has set up a working party to alleviate the gap: a gap I too am now seeking to help fill.

Incidentally, Edward Deci (1995) in *'Why we do what we do'* notes that humanistic psychology evolved out of the psychoanalytic tradition and refers to himself as an "empirical humanist" – based on his use of empirical methods to test his insights into depth psychology and intrinsic motivation. So he and I share a common belief that if an insight is correct, it's possible to demonstrate this scientifically using the techniques of social and even behavioural research.

Our scientific techniques may have been different, but they both constitute scientific methodology. Whilst Deci and his students tend to use anecdotal observations combined with laboratory experiments, I have used anecdotal observations combined with a different quantitative methodology namely statistical analysis of responses to surveys conducted with very large numbers of employees. Another thing Deci and I share is the recognition that extrinsic or external motivation of behaviours (such as reward, punishment, performance objectives etc.) are not as powerful nor as sustained as intrinsic motivation.

Freud also maintained that basic human needs operate on two levels: the conscious, where we know what is going on and why we do things, and the unconscious, where we're only vaguely aware of what is going on, and are unsure of why we do things or why we're happy or unhappy.

This operation of two levels; the conscious or the unconscious; awareness or unawareness, is largely accepted today. For example, individuals talk of their hidden anger, of getting in touch with their 'real self', or of overcoming their inner barriers to success.

Two becomes three

The Capita employee investigation I've described earlier required the development of a reliable and valid measure of motivation/boredom against which to check the impact of possible drivers or causes. To this end, I'd thrown into the survey in no particular order, a comprehensive range of items or statements describing the signals or symptoms (namely behaviours, feelings, sensations, attitudes and emotions) of boredom, recognising that they were probably the inverse identifiers of motivation. For example, "I feel anxious and depressed" is a symptom of boredom but easier to answer accurately than "I feel equable and happy" which is a symptom of motivation. The boredom symptoms had been gathered from my qualitative investigations of the experience of both motivation and boredom (typically group discussions with students, employees and housewives).

In addition I included a selection from over 200 symptoms garnered from the literature on the experience of boredom. Based on a careful review, the symptoms from the literature were able to be rearranged into 21 groups which I called deterioration of performance, attention and mental skills, intellectual capacity and control; sensitivity and childishness; sense of repetition and dullness; sense of constraint and need for release; sense of fatigue; listlessness and loss of interest; lack of satisfaction and pleasure; depression and misery; tension and restlessness; aggression and hostility; anxiety and loss of confidence; self-repression and withdrawal; passivity and politeness; physical sickness and discomfort; coping strategies and focus on trivia; escape strategies and disruptive activities.

Using all this material, the discussions and the literature, I converted the descriptions of boredom symptoms into boredom testing items such as the following:

- 'I often feel restless at work and need to move around just to get a break'
- 'I feel frustrated and fed up at work and just want to leave'
- 'There are times at work when drop off or go on a yawning binge'
- 'I'm pretty quick to pass on extra parts of my job if they come my way'
- 'I find it harder and harder to get out of bed in the morning"
- 'Nothing seems to happen at work, every day is the same'

Similarly, some symptoms were converted into motivation testing items to offer greater variety and to provide balance. Examples of motivation testing items included:

- 'I'm just fascinated by my job, it's really interesting'
- 'At work I feel really confident and in control'
- 'There is a lot of variety in my work, every day is different'

Returning to the Capita investigation and the challenge to develop a measure of employee motivation, the survey responses would be statistically analysed to determine whether they clustered or grouped in any meaningful way. Prior to analysis I could only guess at the results. As mentioned in the last chapter, I hypothesised and confidently expected them to fall into two groups, in line with Freudian theory of two needs or instincts – the sexual (for which I use the term Affiliation) and the aggressive (for which I use the term Achievement).

But then Ron (my statistician) phoned and told me that, instead of identifying two clusters for the symptoms of motivation/boredom, the statistics showed *three.*

The clustering of the motivation symptoms and the boredom symptoms around Freud's two needs or instincts was expected. This also confirmed the motivation/boredom continuum, where symptoms of motivation represent the positive expression of the need and the symptoms of boredom signalled the negative or suppression of the same need. So far so good. But the third need cluster?

I realised there could only be one explanation: it appeared that the data revealed something that Freud had missed. Was it possible that Freud's hypothesis – that a third, higher, human or creative output was a synthesis of the sexual and aggressive needs - wasn't correct? Did creative output instead signal the existence of a separate and independent instinct or need?

When Ron asked if I could explain the results, it required only a slight shift in my Freudian thinking from *two separate instincts or needs plus their combination* to become *three separate instincts or needs*.

Please understand that I'm not claiming to be cleverer than Freud. This advance was made possible by the statistical analysis of survey responses. Freud didn't have access to the two sets of information I had to hand. Firstly, I'd combined over 200 motivation/boredom symptoms into one set of survey questions. And secondly, I'd been able to run the statistics to demonstrate three independent entities.

Reviewing the results of the motivation and boredom testing items, I found the items fell into three groups or clusters denoting three different spectrums of feelings, attitudes and behaviours of motivation/boredom. The first cluster incorporated items describing aspects of interest and of apathy; the second describing aspects of satisfaction and of frustration; and the third describing aspects of commitment and of escapism.

Remembering that the survey items tested for both ends of the motivation/boredom continuum, it was logical that high scores on aspects of interest, satisfaction and commitment meant that the individual scored low scores on aspects of apathy, frustration and escapism; and vice versa. So in conclusion, we now had three needs rather than two; a leap forward on the foundation Freud had initiated.

However, advances in knowledge inevitably come with passing time and new techniques. Freud had developed his concepts based on an analysis of existing literature and through speculative discussions with his patients. The concept of two animal instincts was the accepted biological theory in Freud's day. He made room for our humanness by speculating on the civilising impact of education. Freud believed that the higher human activities – such as creativity, spirituality and altruism – gained their energy from a synthesis of the sexual and aggressive needs. In short, two quite different needs combined in humans to generate the uniquely human aspirations. In my writings, I renamed the sexual need the Affiliate need, and the aggressive need, the Achievement need to ensure the terminology was more in line with the language of business and management.

Serendipitously for me, my research methodology and results demonstrated that the motivation/boredom symptoms fell into three separate and significantly different clusters or factors. This forced a new and exciting conclusion. I reasoned that humans have a third need or instinct, unique to them, and not shared with the animal kingdom as are the other two instincts. Humans have an additional need for a specific and special range of beliefs, activities, achievements and experiences. The higher activities of creativity, altruism, meaning, purpose and spirituality are in fact expressions of this third and uniquely human instinct. Unwittingly, my research had extended Freud's thinking to find a third intrinsic need, one that was not a combination of, or gained its energy from, the other two, but which stood and functioned alone.

So what to call this third need? I leaned towards words such as creative, spiritual, human, altruistic or vocational. However, I came back to Abraham Maslow's (1943) suggestion to call it **Actualisation**, or the expression of the integrated and deepest part of the self. Not only is that a good translation of the many aspects of this human need, it's a term with which many people are familiar.

There are many mysteries surrounding this third need. The other two have a clear, identifiable, physical existence or biological operation.

Affiliation is linked with the sexual, procreation and survival of the species instinct. Achievement is linked with the aggressive, competitive and survival-of-the-individual instinct. But does Actualisation have a physical dimension? I think it is possible. When we think of the creative arts we envision paintings, drama, sculptures, and books. Whilst there is a perhaps higher or invisible element, the Actualisation need is firmly linked to the corporate and physical activities of humans in their educated, spiritual and artistic activities.

In the statistical analysis, the third need clustered separately from the other two but it followed the pattern of the others in grouping the symptoms of the expression of motivation or its suppression, boredom. It underlined that the utilisation or expression of a need, of whatever type, is pleasurable. All the behaviours, feelings and attitudes – such as happiness, satisfaction and ownership – at the positive end of the spectrum are pleasing, whilst the suppression of a need becomes increasingly unpleasant, even painful.

Sharing the insight

I'd become excited when I discovered a new cause of boredom, namely the suppression of verbalisation. However, it didn't compare with the sense of wonder that I experienced when confronted with the apparent evidence of three separate and independent human instincts or needs.

At the time, I was deeply embedded in my studies of Freud and his writings. I searched far and wide amongst Freudian authorities to see if a third independent instinct had been suggested by anyone else. All concurred that the human creative or spiritual activities gained their energy from the two basic sexual and aggressive instincts and its superior nature from the influence of, or modification by, education and civilisation. But if what I'd uncovered were true, then this third instinct was *suis generis* – of its own type – and beholden to no other instinct for its energy, but driven by, or generating, its own energy and motivation.

I longed to share the new insight and first told my husband Neville, but his response was typically calm. Accustomed to my enthusiastic chatter, he saw this as a natural progression of my work: "A prophet in his own country…!" Who else could I tell?

This was too exciting to keep to myself. Down the road from my office was a coffee shop where I met friends and colleagues, and I phoned and arranged a meeting with my academic friend Julia. Then I literally belted off to see her.

Julia was and is a deeply spiritual and religious individual. She's highly intelligent and was then, like me, a postgraduate student and teacher. Perfect! I profess no particular religion and tend to believe in the material world as the beginning and end of our existence, so Julia and I are opposite ends of the spiritual spectrum.

"This is probably the most extraordinary day of my life," I rudely started before she'd opened her mouth. "Let me explain," I continued. "I've run an employee survey in which I included all the symptoms of motivation and boredom that I could find from the literature and my research. These are symptoms of the expression or suppression of our intrinsic needs. They are signs of the way in which we can express and use our instincts and needs."

Julia looked interested and alert. Spilling my coffee, I came straight to the point.

"The symptoms have clustered into *three* groups. This means that beyond the sexual and aggressive drives we share with animals, humans have a separate creative, altruistic or spiritual need. Until now, the received wisdom has been that the spiritual and creative need was simply the educated or more civilised combination of the other two instincts. But my statistical analysis has clearly demonstrated a third spiritual or creative instinct in humans, and *unique* to humans."

Julia leaned back in disappointment. "But that's not new," she said. "The spiritual or creative nature of people is well recognised and accepted. It's certainly part of my experience of life."

Although somewhat deflated, I babbled on. "There's a human instinct or need for the spiritual or creativity – for purpose and meaning that's higher or more important that the basic needs of procreation and survival. It's not just family and work that's important, we all have a higher or more meaningful purpose. You and I have an impulse or need for something higher, something spiritual, altruistic or creative." I was practically waving my arms by this stage. "I've uncovered a third instinct unique to humans and which drives the higher aspirations such as creativity and altruism."

"Really?" she replied. "But I've always known that."

I was stopped in my tracks.

"You might have always 'known' it, but I've just proved it scientifically!" I finally offered. Julia remained unimpressed.

As is invariably the case with the truth, I had 'discovered' what many people had instinctively always known. And indeed, there was from the early 1980s a growing recognition that motivation was not dependent on extrinsic or external stimulus, on reward and punishment, but on intrinsic needs or instincts. This recognition would wait another decade for mainstream acceptance. Intimated by Freud in the early 1900s, and announced by Edward Deci in 1995, the secret of instinct based motivational dynamics has moved from the fringes to the centre of organisational thinking today – a story to be told as we continue through this book.

CHAPTER 3: TOWARDS ME, WE AND IT

The tripartite motivation model

MY EARLY RESEARCH in 1992 uncovered the operation of a third human instinct or need. This led me to formulate my tripartite motivation model which offers a coherent theory of human nature and human dynamics – critically, one validated by empirical research. Over the past 17 years this model has been further confirmed and validated through surveys of over 227,000 employees in a wide range of occupations, working in medium to large Australian and international organisations in both the private and public sector.

The model set out below is constructed around the material from the large-scale Capita survey that used statements denoting the sensations, behaviours and attitudes of the three needs. These symptoms offer an approximation of experience of the three needs, bearing in mind that feelings and behaviours can slide into each other and across the three needs or instincts. For example, good humour may well be in some circumstances a sensation of the expression of the creative drive as well as of the aggressive drive. The allocation of the symptoms (sensations and behaviours) to the three needs is based on the statistical analysis of results and the way they fell onto three factors.

But these clusters may modify slightly across different groups in different circumstances. However, in the essentials they stay firm with the Affiliate drive being responsible for sensations and behaviours associated with interaction and relatedness with other people, the Achievement drive being responsible for those associated with competence and winning and the Actualisation drive being responsible for those associated with meaning and personal purpose.

The theory offers a tripartite-needs-based motivation model. The first two needs are firmly based in our animal nature: namely the needs or instincts for procreation (or sexual drive) and for survival (or aggressive drive), of which the latter is stronger. In modern humans, these basic needs are usually converted from the raw energy of sex and aggression into an infinite range of activities and achievements, where they're expressed in a civilised and educated fashion. The need for procreation often manifests through family or community activities, while survival is seen in sport or professional competition, among other things.

Of greater significance, humans have a need or instinct that goes beyond our animal nature, one that's not shared by the animal kingdom: the need for higher meaning, humanity or personal purpose. The sexual and aggressive needs derive their energy from our animal nature, honed over time into modern human form. However, the third need is exclusive to humanity. Its energy comes from our human nature.

As previously mentioned, Freud hypothesised that our third need was simply a combination of the first two:

> *Based on essentially biological considerations... there are two essentially different classes of instincts: the sexual instincts and the aggressive instincts which are fused towards the achievement of... a higher social value via a process called sublimation.*
>
> – Sigmund Freud (1933) Volume 22, 103 -105

But the evidence from my research is unequivocal: we humans have a third instinct not shared by other members of the animal kingdom.

This "humanity" instinct is what drives individuals to ignore the benefits of money and power and instead to invest their lives into something of "real value", or to "make a difference". It is this instinct that powers extraordinary feats of creativity, courage and compassion, such as choirs and orchestras in prisoner concentration camps, or the services provided by the aid workers and medics of Nobel Peace Prize winner Medécins Sans Frontieres (MSF).

The separation of humans from other members of the animal kingdom by the possession of a creative or altruistic need is a matter of mystery to many people – myself included. Many people prefer the explanation that some form of deity provides the origin and spark for this uniquely human and higher instinct.

Others lean towards a form of Darwinian evolutionary theory, which sees humans developing this unique need or instinct through natural selection, as a process of evolution or survival of the species.

In 2014, I read of the definitive dating – at 40,000 years old – of cave paintings on the Indonesian island of Sulawesi. Investigation team member, archaeologist Thomas Sutikana said: "Rock art is one of the first indicators of an abstract mind – *the onset of being human*, as we know it". Equally old rock art has been discovered in Europe.

My italics emphasise the wide acceptance of a differentiating human need that gives rise to all that we deem most valuable or good in human civilisation – and paradoxically, also to all that we find least valuable or evil in humanity.

In the so-called 'new sciences' of the mind and cognition, a number of authors address the possibility of a third instinct or biological imperative. They use the term morality, or moral cognition (David Brook, 2011; Jonathan Haidt, 2012; Joshua Green, 2014). They seek to explain how this differs from the first two instincts of cooperation and competition, and is "hard-wired" into human cognition and the structure of the brain. For Green, this "moral machinery" includes our capacities for empathy, vengefulness, honour, guilt, embarrassment and righteous indignation. This sort of listing, beloved by many cognitive and behavioural motivation writers, demonstrates the muddle that can arise from not differentiating clearly between the three instincts. Empathy is surely a function of Affiliation or love; vengefulness is surely a function of Achievement or survival.

Let me be clear: in writing this book, I'm not seeking to identify the origin of this third instinct, nor to argue for its origins in any deity, evolutionary development, brain structure or any other hypothesis. This book simply asserts that this third and strongest instinct or need currently exists in humans, and that its level of expression can be identified and measured. Its dynamics of cause and effect, positive and negative, can be tracked and understood – specifically among individuals in a workplace.

This third, higher, instinct is a wondrous and wonderful dimension of humanity. It generates our greatest achievements, inspires our highest aspirations, enlivens our culture and is the source of spirituality. It provides the greatest opportunities for the human race but at the same time offers its greatest challenges.

Challenges of a third need

Let's return to my friend Julia, with whom I'd shared my initial findings about the third need, and my elation over them. My point then, and now, is that "new" wasn't the issue: I'd gathered the evidence to *prove* it. So what did it mean?

I think there are three critical challenges or questions to consider in relation to the third need, which I have named Actualisation:

1. Where does it sit in terms of its strength and forcefulness when compared with the needs of Affiliation and Achievement?

2. What are the implications for individual differences and well-being?

3. How do we ensure that all three needs can be expressed?

To reiterate the evidence and insights to this point: I'd learned that motivation is the opposite of, and exists on a continuum with, boredom. The Capita survey had revealed that symptoms of boredom/motivation separate out and cluster into three sets. These sets demonstrated that humans have three intrinsic instincts or needs, namely sexual or bonding (which I call Affiliate), aggression (Achievement), and meaning (Actualisation).

Figure: Tripartite Motivation: Three Needs

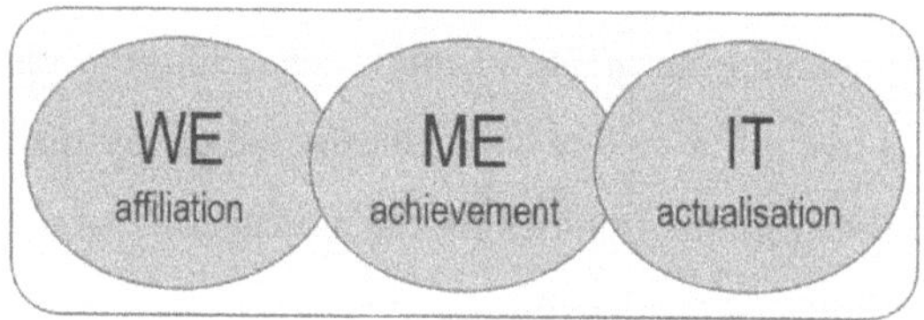

Naming the three needs was a challenge in itself. This was because many of the words I considered were either unfamiliar or altered the meaning slightly. There are a number of labels used by other students of motivation which are more fully explored in a later chapter and collected in the side bar. But best of all the options we considered are those that arose from our casual discussions where 'We, 'Me' and 'It' seemed to capture their essence. These short and catchy labels get the point across, clearly differentiate the three needs and above all are highly memorable.

Intrinsic human need	Label	Need	Satisfier
Sex, procreation, love, interaction, connection	We	Affiliation	People
Aggression, survival, competition, initiative	Me	Achievement	Progress
Creativity, spirituality, vocation, values, meaning	It	Actualisation	Purpose

These three basic instincts or needs are present and operating in all people, but the relative strength of each need may differ according to the individual or situation.

As shown in my tripartite model, the behaviours and feelings experienced when these needs are being met or satisfied are pleasurable and welcome. Where they are being suppressed or denied, then the experience is physically unpleasant, even painful. The expression, or alternatively blocking, of these instincts or needs accounts for the three clusters of positive to negative feelings and behaviours that the research identified – specifically Interest to Apathy; Satisfaction to Frustration; and Commitment to Alienation.

- Interest can include involvement, sense of freedom, variety, cooperation, collaboration, enthusiasm and belonging or membership.
- Satisfaction can include good humour, focus, positivity, challenge, flexibility, pride in your work, responsiveness and a sense of mastery.
- Commitment can include expression, creativity, innovation, a sense of purpose and meaning, responsibility and ownership.

Brought together, the difference between a motivated individual and a bored or de-motivated individual is startling; and explains why we care so much that we and our partners or colleagues are motivated rather than not.

Figure: Behaviours and attitudes in the motivation-boredom continuum

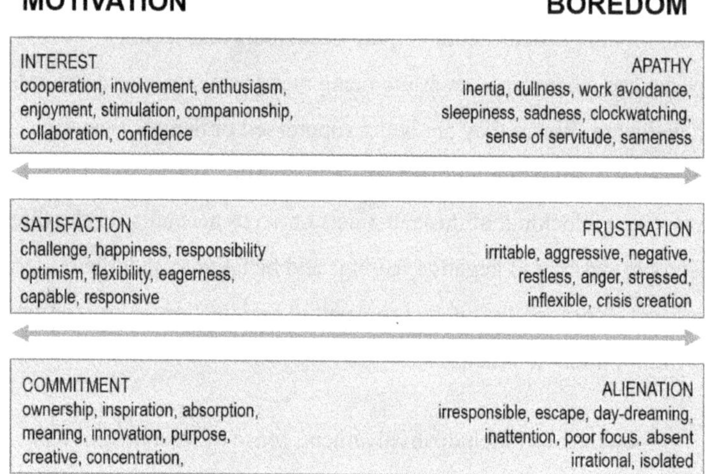

MOTIVATION
BOREDOM
INTEREST
cooperation, involvement, enthusiasm, enjoyment, stimulation, companionship, collaboration, confidence
APATHY
inertia, dullness, work avoidance, sleepiness, sadness, clockwatching, sense of servitude, sameness
SATISFACTION
challenge, happiness, responsibility optimism, flexibility, eagerness, capable, responsive
FRUSTRATION
irritable, aggressive, negative, restless, anger, stressed, inflexible, crisis creation
COMMITMENT
ownership, inspiration, absorption, meaning, innovation, purpose, creative, concentration,
ALIENATION
irresponsible, escape, day-dreaming, inattention, poor focus, absent irrational, isolated

Challenge one: the hierarchy of needs

This brings us back to the three challenges. Where does Actualisation sit in terms of its strength and forcefulness when compared with Affiliation and Achievement?

I maintain that they exist in this order of ascending strength:

1. WE: Procreation or the sexual need; expressed at work as Affiliation or bonding.

2. ME: Survival or aggressive need; expressed at work as Achievement or competition.

3. IT: Meaning or human need; expressed at work as Actualisation or creativity.

How do we know that the instinct my research has uncovered – the human, or creative, need – is the strongest?

It's a biological fact that the survival instinct is stronger than the instinct for procreation. We know that reproduction is abandoned in the face of a threat to survival – the individual's desire to survive is stronger than its drive to procreate. The symptoms of boredom support this – apathy is a milder form of boredom than frustration. In turn, the severest form of boredom – the one associated with the human instinct – is that of escape and alienation. There's even independent research to confirm this.

In what is a surprisingly little known or non-referenced study conducted in 1954, three psychologists namely Bexton, Heron and Scott, interested in what happened in war time experiences, demonstrated that over time boredom increased in severity. The researchers observed these stages by putting volunteer subjects into isolation cells inducing sensory deprivation. They observed increasing deterioration into deeper and more severe boredom. Rather like a whirlpool going down a drain, the stages of boredom past through first the Affiliate or We boredom of apathy, sadness or loneliness. Then it progressed to the Achievement or Me boredom of irritation, frustration, and loss of focus or skills. Finally, it moved to the Actualisation or It boredom which involved hallucinations, alienation, body detachment and desire to escape.

The researchers noted that towards the third stage, the subjects would abandon the experiment and get out! Of course the researchers were not aware at that time of the issue of motivation or its three types. They simply observed the worsening and increasingly uncomfortable sensations and behaviours of individuals, in this case volunteer university students, in response to an environment of isolation induced boredom.

The experiment has been repeated since in 1962 and was reported by Dr S Smith of Lancaster Moor Hospital in his 'clinical aspects of perceptual isolation'. "Our observations and records outline a fairly clear-cut chain of events. At first most volunteers show a tendency to sleep for a long time, then there follows a period of growing agitation, tension and restlessness. Then it moves to disturbed or delusional thinking with most subjects experiencing panic and leaving the room".

In conclusion, on the motivation scale, interest signals lower intensity motivation than satisfaction, which in turn lags behind the highest or strongest form of motivation, which is commitment or purpose. The truth of this hierarchy is manifest not only at work, but in many areas of life. It may explain such behaviours as "starving in a garret for the sake of art". Certainly, we know that relationships flicker to life because of mutual interest, are strengthened by satisfaction, and reach their apex through commitment or purpose.

The emotions, sensations and behaviours of the strongest motivation, the human or creative need is quantifiably and qualitatively different from the sensations and behaviours of the other two needs. They are separated not by streams or rivers, but by oceans. Only forces of such quality and strength could be responsible for both the greatest opportunities and greatest challenges facing the human race.

Challenge two: implications for individual differences

The second challenge concerns the implications of the three needs for individual differences and well-being.

In the Capita research, I included additional material to develop statistically derived attitudinal profiles from the over 1500 employees surveyed. Comparing profiles by their motivation results, it was clear that certain profiles or types of employees had stronger tendencies for one of the three needs. Some employees were experiencing higher or lower scores on the different needs at the time of the survey.

First: the 'We' type of employee – whom I labelled the Citizen – was mainly troubled by the lack of opportunity for group interaction and the expression of his or her need for Affiliation.

Second: the 'Me' type of employee – whom I labelled the Individual – was mainly troubled by the lack of opportunity for new career-enhancing projects and the expression of their need for Achievement.

Third: the 'It' type of employee - whom I labelled the Escapist - was most troubled by their company purpose or ethics and the expression of their need for Actualisation.

(As the name suggests, Escapists either left or wanted to leave to pursue a more meaningful activity.)

It's critical to understand that all three types of employees possessed all three needs. It was current circumstances interacting with their personalities that brought one particular need into prominence at the time of the survey. Given a different timing of the survey, the dominant need might have changed and the employee might fall into a different motivational profile.

It's also noteworthy that the negative end of the continuum describes behaviours, feelings and attitudes which, if entrenched or unrelieved, would qualify as pathologies. There is extensive literature on the "bored" personality and the link between boredom, depression and suicide. But that is a different discussion for a different author in a different book! My understanding is that the reasons why people move from temporary boredom into pathological boredom is related to early development, trauma or even brain injury. I best hold to the area where I'm more suited. My topic is the understanding of motivation and boredom as dynamic, temporary and changing conditions at work or play.

Challenge three: ensuring all needs are met

The third and perhaps most important challenge is finding the conditions under which an expressive life can flourish – in other words, the causes or drivers of motivation.

For the Capita research, a full range of drivers, causes and antecedents of both motivation and boredom were culled or lifted from employee focus groups and the literature. These were sorted and translated into 45 testing statements.

I speculated that the causes or drivers of boredom at work would fall into two categories, namely monotony (the widely accepted version) or suppression of expression, specifically verbal (illustrated by my Eureka moment). I speculated that the drivers of motivation would be the opposite, namely variety or freedom of expression. Again, I was in for a surprise.

Statistical analysis looked for groupings of drivers and to identify those that were highly correlated with the motivation/boredom conditions. The drivers initially fell into two groups: first, manager or leadership, and second, company culture. However, neither pointed to simply monotony or lack of verbalisation.

In terms of the leadership/manager group, the drivers of motivation were a balance of freedom of expression, confidence and aspirations in a well-planned and managed environment. The drivers of boredom included constraints on verbal expression, barriers to confidence and self-esteem and aspirations, as well as poor management and planning

In terms of the company culture group, the drivers of motivation were a balance between freedom of expression, individuality, and aspirations with an ordered, well-designed, quality workplace. The drivers of boredom included stops on verbal expression, individuality and aspirations, in addition to bureaucratic processes and emphasis on quantity over quality.

So the key to motivation is finding **optimal levels of organisation or structure in balance with freedom of expression**. Excessive freedom – a license to do anything – isn't the answer. The definition I offered in an article in the book New Directions in Management (1994) still holds true:

'Employee motivation is a condition of interest, satisfaction and purpose that occurs as a result of workplace order and structure in combination with encouragement of individual freedom of expression, dignity and aspirations'.

My subsequent investigations over many years have simply confirmed or increased in nuance the potency of environmental conditions, where freedom or autonomy is balanced with supportive and humane systems and controls.

In coming chapters, I'll review the results of my subsequent work with client companies. This produced sufficient evidence to increase the number of elements impacting motivation and to define a pragmatic set of drivers or causes that operate in the workplace. Identifying these drivers was essential. Merely suggesting that a company must try to strike a balance between freedom and control doesn't provide enough guidance for it to take action. My further investigations were aimed at identifying scientifically the programs, processes or actions that would provide the necessary balance of freedom and order to ensure that employees were motivated.

The drivers of employee motivation I identified fall into seven action areas and these are described and discussed at length in a later Chapter called 'The Drivers of Motivation'. Readers interested primarily in workplace motivation might prefer to skip ahead.

The essence of my theory

Now for a quick review of my tripartite motivation model. My research had demonstrated:

- Motivation is the opposite of and exists on a continuum with boredom

- Symptoms (behaviours, feelings and attitudes) of boredom/motivation separate out into three sets

- The three sets are consistent with humans having three intrinsic needs, namely Affiliate (bonding), Achievement (aggression) and Actualisation (meaning) – which I often describe as We, Me and It.

- Laboratory studies have shown that the three needs increase in strength and potency – from affiliation, through aggression to actualisation.

- The expression or alternatively blocking of these needs accounts for three clusters of positive to negative feelings and behaviours, namely interest to apathy; satisfaction to frustration and commitment to alienation

- By looking at the motivation scores of different types of employees, we find that whilst the three needs operate in all people, the relative strength of each may differ according to personality, time or situation

- Interaction with people (**We**) is necessary to meet the need for **Affiliation**, friendship, connection, community, affection, and even love. A sense of progress (**Me**) is necessary to meet the needs of **Achievement**, winning, challenge, success, or individual recognition. And most exciting of all, a sense of higher purpose (**It**) is necessary to meet the needs of **Actualisation,** meaning, creativity, passion or spirituality.

- Further examination of survey results demonstrates that the environment necessary to drive or enhance motivation requires a combination of freedom within boundaries or supportive controls.

- This freedom within structure (order) rule applies whether it relates to the behaviours and style of management or leadership or relates to the organisational culture.

A rose by any other name

Over the years I've used various terms to name or describe the three human needs or instincts, changing as I've learned more, read more and progressively better understood their nature. These terms have been gathered from the literature or my own research; and are obviously interchangeable. Labels may have more meaning for some individuals rather than others.

Some labels have been borrowed from other authors and some I've selected for the purposes of explanation and exposition. The table below offers many of those that are currently used or seem to ring a bell in workshops and training groups. Where attribution to specific authors is possible (not all have offered three but sometimes four or five needs) I've done so in a later chapter.

In naming the three needs, at the time of writing, I've settled on the first set of 'Affiliation, Achievement and Actualisation'. However, the most recent more colloquial set, 'We, Me and It' best conveys their meaning to most people and importantly are the easiest to remember!

The first need is to be part of, and to operate within, a group, team or family of other people - hence the term "We".

The second need is to take oneself as one's primary concern in exercising individual talents and achieving a winning position – it's all about "Me".

The third need is for something out there, something bigger than me or the group; something that means one can make a difference or contribute to something important for every individual – the hard-to-define "It".

'We, Me and It' are easy for everyone to remember and surprisingly accurate in defining the needs or instincts.

More recently a colleague suggested another set of alliterative labels: Connect, Challenge and Create. In essence, the terminology selected can be any that helps to define and understand the nature of and the differences between the three instincts or needs.

There are probably many more and as a reader you might like to add some that you think hit the mark. Developing your own names will assist in the process of internalisation and ownership of the very useful knowledge about motivation and its tripartite nature and dynamics.

Freud's original two instincts	Sexual	Aggressive	Synthesis of sexual and aggressive
Hinds' Tripartite needs	Affiliation	Achievement	Actualisation
Easy labels	WE	ME	IT
Other labels/ Synonyms	Procreation Connect Communication Love People Cooperation Membership	Survival Challenge Competition War Progress Disagreement Mastery	Spirituality Create Values Civilisation Purpose Vocation Meaning

CHAPTER 4: A COMPLEX PHENOMENON

The story so far...

THROUGH TELLING THE STORY of my research and work, I've taken you on an unusual journey to examine, and acknowledge, the importance of motivation to ourselves and others, at home, at work and at play. Initially attempting to study motivation in the educational context, I found that students speak more readily of their experiences of boredom. As a result, I pursued the concept of boredom as a possible entry point to student motivation and perhaps employee motivation. However, I was disconcerted to find the almost total lack of scientific or academic interest in the topic of boredom and its conceptual separation from the topic of motivation.

Replicating this neglect, I noted the denial of the experience of boredom in social situations and at work. I speculated that this neglect might well be linked to the wide range of very unpleasant or even painful emotions and behaviours experienced in the stat e of boredom. At the same time, I noted that the accepted wisdom was that boredom in both school and work - or wherever - is simply caused by the lack of stimulation or monotony.

Despite the fact that boredom was not a focus of scientific study, etymological evidence confirmed that boredom is a constant in the lives of men and women as found in literature through the ages. It was therefore a problem worth pursuing!

From my personal eureka moment, I gained the insights that first boredom operated on a continuum with motivation and that second the suppression of the need to disagree is an alternative and perhaps more significant cause than just monotony. This anecdotal experience needed to be scientifically tested, so I designed a research investigation to test first, the links between motivation and boredom and second, the potency of the cause of the suppression of individual opinion.

Scientific evidence was sought by means of a full workplace survey of more than 1500 employees. The inclusion of the more readily recognisable symptoms (behaviours and sensations) of boredom strengthened the accuracy of the motivation measure, which was able to record the full positive-to-negative range of this human experience. The results confirmed my insights that motivation operated on a continuum with boredom, specifically along two known instincts where interest contrasts with apathy and satisfaction contrasts with frustration. The survey confirmed a second cause or driver of motivation/boredom beyond stimulation and monotony – namely the expression or suppression of individual opinion or verbalisation.

However, my statistician offered me a challenge that motivation incorporated not two but three innate needs. To solve this problem, I delved a little deeper into the psychological studies and writings of the needs-based theorists (or humanist tradition). Noting the conflict between behaviourists and needs-based theorists, I opted to take up the latter approach to explain the findings. By adding scientific evidence to the needs-based theories, I join the group of “empirical humanists” as coined in 1995 by Edward L. Deci.

My challenge to define three, as opposed to two, innate needs was met by extending the Freudian theory of two instincts – Sexual and Aggressive – into three. I offered the names Affiliation, Achievement and Actualisation (the short hand version We, Me and It seems to work best for most people). Sharing the insight of the existence of a uniquely human third instinct or need for spirituality, altruism, creativity, or meaning didn’t get any applause because its existence in everyday experience was taken for granted. Never the less, it is the need that defines the best in humanity and has been known throughout recorded history.

These findings supported the development of a tripartite motivation model of human motivation/boredom identifying the three needs Affiliation, Achievement and Actualisation and their manifestation into three sets of experiences, namely “interest versus apathy”, “satisfaction versus frustration” and “commitment versus alienation” (including their characteristic attitudes and behaviours).

A further examination of the nature of the instincts or needs confirmed the complexity of the dynamics of human motivation. First there is a hierarchy of needs with an ascending order of strength; second there are different manifestations of one need over another in different people at different times; and third ensuring that all three needs are met in the workplace requires an environment – not easy to achieve – which has the right balance of freedom embedded within structure.

Intrinsic or extrinsic motivation?

I have traced the conflict, experienced on a personal as well as theoretical levels, between two psychological schools of thought. The behaviourists, who focus exclusively on extrinsic motivation (as stimulated or controlled by such things as goals, rewards and punishments), and needs-based theorists or the humanist tradition, who deem intrinsic motivation as more significant.

Extrinsic motivation is predicated on some source of incentive or stimulus that arrives from the external world. Reward and punishment are the most obvious sources of extrinsic motivation. For many years, it was assumed that pay and reward for performance was all that was needed to ensure sufficient effort from workers. Similarly, school children were driven by demand, threat and often corporal punishment. External stimulus is the most obvious way of controlling another's behaviour – it is the basis of training dogs. However, external stimulus can have a short or contradictory impact. And is not suited to inducing behaviour that is not easily measured: think customer service, innovation, caring or problem-solving. As they say "You cannot legislate for a smile". There is even evidence that extrinsic incentives can actually undermine true or sustained motivation (Deci and Ryan, 2002).

So intrinsic motivation is the way to go. However, intrinsic motivation is no simple thing. The three needs provide the energy for all human interaction, action and existence, but motivation remains a mystery because the combined needs find expression in myriad ways across many feelings, behaviours, sensations, actions and relationships. How we experience and express our needs is informed by our circumstances, education, culture, individual personality, geography and more.

However, all our actions, feelings and experiences are some form of expression of all three basic motivational needs: people are not separated by having one need instead of another. It's possible to experience the operation of one need more strongly at one moment, but all three must be answered and none can be neglected or ignored. For instance, in the workplace, employees need colleagues or a team for affiliation, opportunities for promotion or new projects for achievement, and the attachment of meaning, purpose and creativity to their work for actualisation.

It's difficult if not impossible to observe the separation of the three needs because they operate concurrently and in interaction with each other. They combine and synthesise to provide the motivating force or energy brought to jobs, responsibilities and tasks. The salient point is that corporate leaders can't assume that answering one need – for instance achievement by way of winning sales – is enough to keep an employee motivated. Every human has a loving/community self, an aggressive/competitive self and a creative/spiritual self. This is our basic humanity, and the source of the complex motivations that drive our loyalty, effort and commitment.

I am, of course, talking about *intrinsic* – in-built – motivation. For some theorists, specifically the self-determination folk, motivation is *only* intrinsic, but I firmly believe that external sources can modify the arousal or repression of inner motivation. My research into the impact of workplace drivers demonstrates that there's a continuous and important interplay between intrinsic needs and the external world, which stimulates or represses the expression of these needs. This interplay in the workplace is more fully explored in the next chapter of this book.

Child's play

Understanding the three types of motivation is easier and clearer when we consider children at play.

Imagine if you will a crowd of children at the beach or seaside, free to play on the wide golden sand. In a typical panorama of my country, Australia, the children are in their bathers or swimsuits and have the usual balls, buckets and spades. It's an idyllic scene.

One group decides to join together to build a sandcastle. They set about it busily, in complete harmony. They make a design circle, shovel the sand and watch the castle grow. No one has given them directions. They've formed a group and are talking and making suggestions whilst building. It's a perfect illustration of teamwork and the operation of the need for bonding; a living picture of the Affiliation motivation, the "We", and an example of happy children.

But things change. Suddenly one child gets tired of the group play and wants to show off, to be superior and different. He runs from a distance and takes a flying leap onto the castle, exulting in this show of strength and shouting out "I'm the king of the castle!" This of course ruins the castle – but perhaps for him, running and jumping on sandcastles is more satisfying, and makes him feel powerful and a winner. This is an illustration of the operation of the need for individuality, independence and aggression. It's a picture of the Achievement motivation, the "Me", and an example of a satisfied and exultant child.

Finally, we see one child at a distance from the others. This solitary boy is contentedly creating his own small sand garden, decorated with shells and seaweed. He's humming and stays engrossed in creating his sand pictures, without being aware of time passing. This is an illustration of the operation of the need for knowledge, creativity, purpose and meaning. It's a picture of the Actualisation motivation, the "It", and of a contented or inspired child.

Each of the three needs are set in motion by an object or goal – to build a castle, to destroy a castle or to make a garden. The object or goal is the focus of the motivational energy in all of us which can be applied to a myriad of other goals or objects.

Any time we're at the beach, we can see in the play of children – and indeed of adults – the expression of the three needs for bonding, aggression and meaning: of the needs for Affiliation, Achievement and Actualisation. When these needs are being expressed, we can expect to observe individuals who are happy, satisfied or absorbed. At different times and in different beachgoers, the three conditions are always evident.

Democracy, authoritarianism and anarchy

In the late 1970s, much was made of the concept of the "democratic company", or bringing democratic participation into the workplace. As with many business-management theories, this largely made way for other ideas (although the workplace freedom/democracy movement persists to this day specifically in the Nordic countries).

My point in raising this is that different forms of government offer a useful model of the nature and conditions necessary for promoting human (and specifically employee) motivation in organisations.

I want to tell you about a real-time documentary film I saw in the late 1970s whilst studying for my MA in education at Macquarie University. The film was made in Poland to illustrate Kurt Lewin's field force analysis and humanist theory about the impact of social forces on the individual's behavior and personality. Lewin (1890–1947) was a German–American psychologist and a pioneer in social, organisational and applied psychology. He coined the term "group dynamics" and suggested that an organisation's management and culture are defined by one of three leadership styles: authoritarian, democratic or laissez-faire. Lewin suggested that individuals behave in response to environmental factors that are either *helping forces*, which drive movement or motivation towards a goal; or *hindering forces*, which block movement or motivation. The term *helping forces* later became Deci's 'autonomy supporting environment'

The Lewin-inspired documentary solidified my own model of intrinsic motivation and its dynamics. In spite of the film's Polish-language dialogue, which was incomprehensible to me, it was clear and compelling, and I vividly recall its impact. The film is shot in a specially constructed set with walls radiating from a central point and three doors connecting the three rooms thus formed. Each room has a long table at which are seated five or six boys and girls of about seven years of age.

The film opens in the "democratic" room (i.e. autonomy supporting environment), where a female teacher enters with a basket containing plasticine of many different colours. She tells the children that they're going to make things for an Easter display. The children are excited. "What type of things?" they ask. She responds seeking their opinion, and they suggest Easter eggs, bunnies, flowers and even fish. She says: "Whatever you think goes with Easter." One boy asks if he can make things for Christmas and the teacher replies that the aim today is for Easter – it's not Christmas yet. The boy seems satisfied with the answer.

The teacher puts the plasticine on the table, invites the children to select what they want and tells them that she'll return in 10 minutes to see how they're going. She reminds them to help each other, to share the colours and that they can talk about what they're doing. The children start at once. They choose plasticine and tell each other about their ideas. Some start making things quickly while others think a little longer about what they want to do, but all have started by the time the teacher leaves the room.

Upon entering the "authoritarian" room (in Deci's terms the 'controlling environment'), the same teacher follows the same procedure, but this time changes her demeanor and is less benign and more directive. She instructs the children to each use only one colour and to make only Easter eggs. The children are nevertheless eager to begin – it looks like fun. Then the teacher adds some more instructions. The children are to make as many eggs as possible and avoid talking; they should work quickly and quietly. She says she will check on progress in 10 minutes. This doesn't appear to detract from the novelty or challenge and all the children begin work with apparent pleasure.

In the "laissez-faire" or permissive room (in Deci's terms the 'inconsistent or chaotic environment') the teacher again follows the same procedure but invites the children to make whatever they like. She doesn't impose any limitations about time or sharing. When asked about making something not for Easter, she replies that they're free to choose for themselves. Again the children are eager to begin but they lose time as they grab and jostle for their share of the plasticine.

The film then moves with the teacher from room to room. On her second visit to the democratic room, she helps the children with their choices, comments on their progress, praises their efforts and when asked, offers guidance or suggestions. She helps them to share, to avoid conflicts over access to colours and suggests making more objects as each one is finished. The children are clearly engrossed and the time flies. When the teacher asks them to stop on her third and final visit, there's a splendid display of a diverse range of beautiful Easter decorations to show for their efforts, made as they talked and cooperated. It's a scene of great variety, accomplishment and creativity.

On the teacher's second visit to the authoritarian room, there's evidence of progressively deepening boredom and monotony. She reminds the children to hurry up, not to use other colours and to make only eggs. When children ask to change colours or make other things they're firmly told no. Their movements slow and fewer eggs are made as time passes. The audible sighs and murmurings of boredom, apathy and monotony are met with warnings from the teacher. On her final visit, the camera pans across rows of identical eggs in serried ranks. Though uniform, the eggs are fewer in total than the decorations in the democratic room. It's a scene of careful construction, uniform output and fewer objects completed.

On the teacher's second and final visits to the laissez-faire room the scene becomes progressively more chaotic. She appears not to care what happens, and avoids or ignores most of the children. Some children try to make objects but they gradually stop work. Difficulties and tension increase. Finally, two boys start throwing the plasticine around. The teacher doesn't interfere, and the behavior turns towards intimidation and bullying. A child asks to leave; others break down into tears. In one particularly memorable sequence a silent, wide-eyed boy stands back against a wall, white faced with confusion and distress. The final laissez-faire room scene is one of utter destruction. Plasticine is spread across the table and only one or two of the few objects made are left intact.

The film depicts freedom integrated with structure (in the democracy room) in contrast to excessive control (authoritarian) or permissiveness (laissez-faire). For Lewin, this demonstrated the virtues of democracy versus authoritarianism and revolution. For me, it was a graphic illustration of my research findings: a motivating environment balances freedom with structure to promote intrinsic motivation as an expression of the three needs for Affiliation, Achievement and Actualisation. Both the absence of freedom (controlling) and excessive freedom (or permissiveness - chaotic) block or undermine the expression of needs and produce boredom, apathy, aggression and alienation.

A word about the impact of permissiveness. It's fairly clear why a *lack* of freedom can repress or obstruct the expression of intrinsic needs. But what happens when there's *too much* freedom? Simply, when things are out of control, fear or flight (possibly psychic) takes over. The reflex response for many is to freeze; for others it's fight or flight – which the film shows. The children's reactions prevented the useful and civilised expression of intrinsic needs.

Given optimum conditions for full expression of all three human needs, the resulting behaviours and achievements are many and varied – so much so that they account for all the wonders of human civilisation, education and history. It's easy to see that human motivation is highly complex and difficult to pin down as it has so many manifestations. Hence it is simpler to recognise de-motivation and boredom. Their behaviours are more limited and more painful. It's easier to recognise and describe feelings of loneliness, sadness, depression and anger than to pin down the feelings of love, accomplishment, euphoria, focus or inspiration. For these reasons, symptoms of boredom often operate as more accurate measures of motivation/boredom in surveys or questionnaires.

All this may be very clear if it's presented in a film or we see a motivated group in action. It becomes more difficult when we're trying to introduce the preconditions of employee motivation into our team or company. Here, fortunately, a little science has come to the rescue. As well as demonstrating that freedom combined with control provides the necessary conditions for employee motivation, my workplace Capita research identified the practical programs, actions and processes that satisfy the definition of a motivating environment. I didn't have to convert abstract ideas of "autonomy within structure" or "freedom within control" into reality: my research identified them. Additional research surveys over the years and across many organisations further defined and progressively updated the activities that support, trigger or drive employee intrinsic motivation. Performance on these drivers or actions determines the extent to which employees are motivated and engaged.

What does it all mean for you?

The application of information and knowledge to one's own life constitutes the getting of wisdom. Understanding employee motivation and its pre-conditions on the basis of research, information and insights is all very well. But using this knowledge to be helpful in the wiser conduct of our own lives – both at work *and* play – is more of a challenge.

The three needs provide three sources of energy that are always available to you. These energy sources intertwine, synthesise, modify and support each other like sections of an orchestra, with variations and interplay of different needs being dominant at different times and in different situations.

However, each need and its energy requires three conditions to become active:

An **object** (goal, task or activity) towards which the need can be directed (e.g. I want to be the best salesperson)

A **structure** (path, set of rules or parameters) to guide and manage the energy, ensure it achieves its objective and prevents dissipation or waste of impetus (e.g. I operate within the company guidelines and use their sales systems)

And finally **freedom**, choice and opportunity to engage with the object (e.g. I can define and engage with my potential customers the way I want)

Successful expression of your intrinsic energies always requires these conditions operating both externally and internally. You may experience external prohibitions and lack the necessary freedom of choice through lack of authority, time, resources, or money. On the other hand, these prohibitions may be operating internally. Intrinsic restrictions are the habits, experiences and learning influences from which we've taken rules and incorporated them into our thinking and even personality. It's these rules – not the outside world – that can often prevent us taking the path to express our needs.

Thinking of my own Eureka experience where a situation of interest turned into a condition of boredom, there was in reality nothing external to stop me speaking my mind in the lecture hall. My own internalised rules of courtesy laid down the barriers against expressing my disagreement. It could be argued that I had good reason to stay silent. But remember, I was at a university, where freedom of opinion is meant to be valuable. No one would have carted me off to prison if I'd put up my hand to disagree.

There are occasions when you can't, for external or internal reasons, express your needs and their energies. If this is the case, then you're likely to experience boredom or apathy, frustration or dissatisfaction, and distraction or the need for escape. To turn these experiences into interest, satisfaction and sense of meaning or purpose, it's necessary to consider where the blocks are occurring. Sometimes the lack of freedom or lack of permission is buried deep in our personality and some form of external assistance is needed to free us from entrenched boredom or depression. More usually, energy blocks can be fixed by truthful consideration of the situation. Seeking to understand the source of the blockage provides an opportunity to alleviate the issue. Setting a goal, gaining the skills, learning the rules and giving oneself permission or time to pursue the goal is the high road to a motivating and engaging life.

The rewards of such an approach are self-evident. Boredom with one's occupation need not necessarily point to a job change: it can mean an adjustment to one's situation, opportunities and roles. And boredom in a marriage needn't necessarily lead to a divorce – it can instead be an insight into how the partnership needs to readjust its dynamics, roles, responsibilities or communication.

It may be helpful to self-evaluate your motivation or lack of it.

Figure: Tripartite Motivation Model

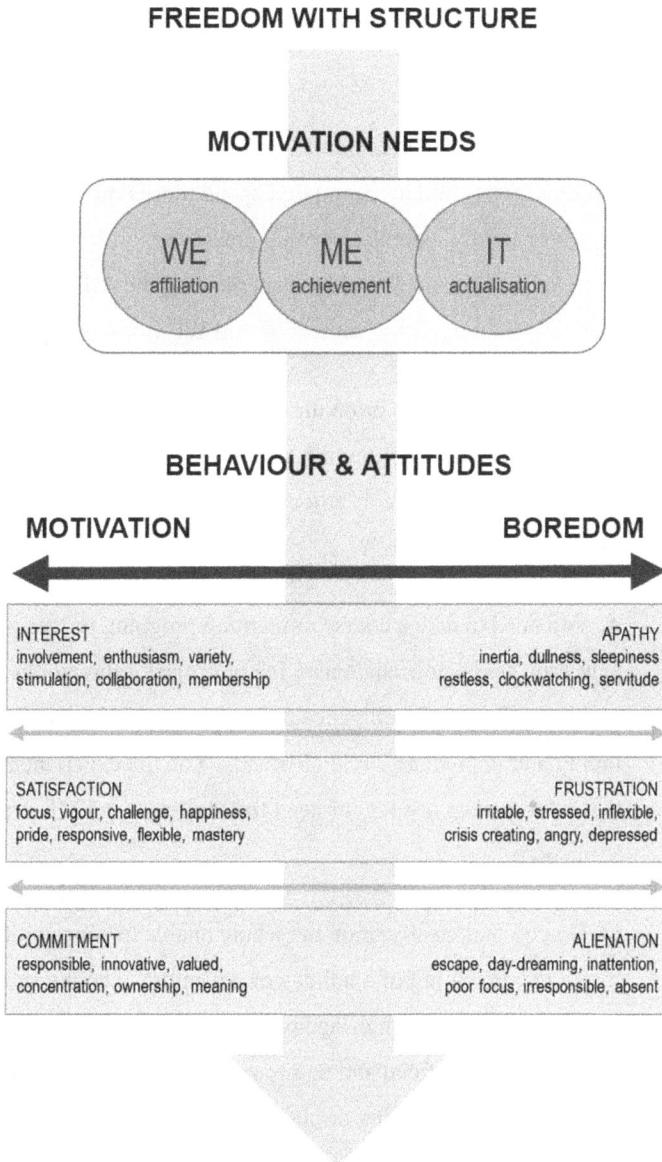

FREEDOM WITH STRUCTURE

MOTIVATION NEEDS

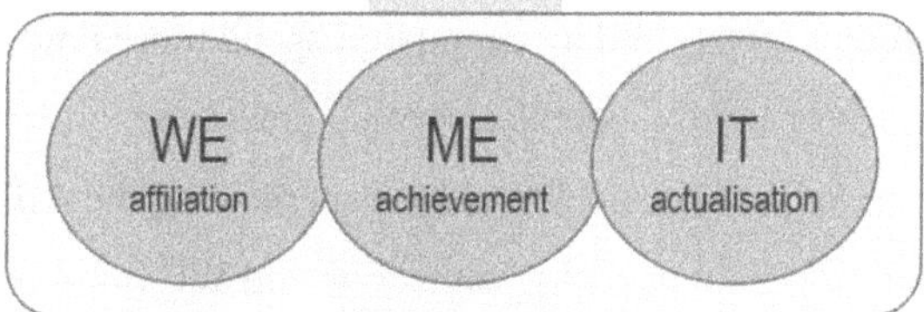

BEHAVIOUR & ATTITUDES

MOTIVATION	BOREDOM
INTEREST involvement, enthusiasm, variety, stimulation, collaboration, membership	APATHY inertia, dullness, sleepiness restless, clockwatching, servitude
SATISFACTION focus, vigour, challenge, happiness, pride, responsive, flexible, mastery	FRUSTRATION irritable, stressed, inflexible, crisis creating, angry, depressed
COMMITMENT responsible, innovative, valued, concentration, ownership, meaning	ALIENATION escape, day-dreaming, inattention, poor focus, irresponsible, absent

If you are having negative feelings or experiencing boredom, you can identify which of your needs is being suppressed.

Q. Do you feel mostly or on the whole sad, bored, lacking in interest, unhappy, dull, enslaved, sleepy, uninvolved, or apathetic?

A. You need to find greater interaction with people, seek to be part of a group, find a community, spend more time with my friends or family, volunteer or find greater opportunity for team or group participation. You are experiencing the Affiliation need, and your need for connection and WE is not being met.

Q. Do you feel mostly or on the whole bad tempered, depressed, irritated, aggressive, pessimistic, restless, angry, stubborn, unchallenged or unfocussed? Are you tending to say, "that's not my problem"?

A. You need to take a course or learning program, to gain a new skill, find a new challenge, job or project, reinvigorate my career, or use your intelligence and abilities outside your family and immediate circle of friends. You are experiencing the Achievement need, your need for challenge and ME is not being met.

Q. Do you feel mostly or on the whole unable to concentrate, distracted, dreaming of a holiday or adventure, wanting to get up and leave my job, marriage or situation? Are you feeling that you are superficial and unimportant, irresponsible, or that life is lacking in meaning or purpose?

A. You need to seek out the meaning of your life, listen to your inner voice, take up a new hobby or creative activity, or seek greater spirituality. You need to do something you have always wanted to do – establish a bucket list and do the first thing on that list *now*. You need to be honest with yourself, work out who you are and review whether anything in your past has led you down the wrong path for you. You are experiencing the Actualisation need, your need for meaning and IT is not being met.

This last and strongest need, the It, is often the most urgent and the most difficult to satisfy. It takes courage, self-confidence and a belief in oneself to become a painter instead of a merchant banker, do the garden instead of mopping the floors, or forge a new path instead of doing what is expected of you. But satisfying "It", or finding purpose, doesn't have to be world beating, important or publicly impressive. You're on course as long as you believe it's something finer, has meaning, is uniquely yours, or makes a difference.

The best advice I can give any individual, based on my learning and experience, is to use the experience of boredom to make changes for oneself and *not to blame others or the world for the problem*. In the words of Cassius (Shakespeare, Julius Caesar Act I). *"The fault, dear Brutus, is not in our stars, but in ourselves..."*

Feelings, behaviours and signals

My workplace surveys over time have demonstrated the three needs operating in all participants: all humans share the same needs for love, achievement and meaning. But we don't share these needs equally, at all times and in all situations.

Survey data from more than 227,000 employees working in different industries and workplaces showed that different people experience one drive more strongly than another at different times, and that the feelings we experience will signal to us which one of the three needs is currently being blocked or satisfied. Over time, I got to know these indicators, and gave the people experiencing them fun names for convenience sake. Here's a snapshot of what they look like.

BOREDOM: ARE YOU SAD, BAD OR MAD?

SAD employees claim a lack interest, lack of involvement, clock watching, sleepiness, inertia and sadness: they're experiencing the "apathy" type of boredom. The 'Sads' seek connection, warmth, human exchange, friendship, social contact, physical comfort or well-being, and the pleasantries or minor dramas of family-type interrelationships. Sad employees are feeling disconnected and alone. Their need for Affiliation (the We) is being blocked or denied.

BAD employees claim to experience pessimism, a sense of being fed up, anger, depression, irritation and a preference for crises or disruptive activities: they're experiencing the "frustration" type of boredom. 'Bads' seek verbalisation of criticism and opinions, the opportunity to analyse problems, transparent systems supporting achievement and good organisation. They often demand the introduction of more equitable, rational or ethical workplace processes. They're feeling frustrated and angry. Their need for Achievement (the Me) is being blocked or denied.

MAD employees claim to experience a sense of non-connectedness and distraction. They seek escapist activities like daydreaming, planning a holiday, searching the internet or reading, and can often feel sleepy or inattentive: they're experiencing the "alienation" type of boredom. 'Mads' look for creative play or a personally enriching activity that gives them an opportunity for imaginative expression. They seek cultural activities and creativity and if they can't find these at work, they'll look for them outside work, or with another employer. They're feeling driven to distraction and longing to escape. Their need for Actualisation (the It) is being blocked or denied.

In line with the differential strength of the needs, sad is less severe than bad, which is less severe than mad.

Of course, many people prefer not to consider boredom and its negative connotations (look at the current popularity of positive psychology, with its focus on the "upside" instead of the pathology or negative). So the positive indicators are crucial.

MOTIVATION: ARE YOU HAPPY, CLAPPY OR ZAPPY?

HAPPY employees are the opposite of sad and claim to be interested, warm, engaged, cooperative, having a sense of variety, and feeling involved and light-hearted. The success of social media attests to a current demand for happiness – but happiness is a sensation linked to *being with people*. It's the opposite of loneliness and isolation. Affiliation motivation is experienced when the need for affection, interaction and bonding is met. But being happy will not provide complete fulfillment as it ignores the other two needs.

CLAPPY employees are the opposite of bad and its associated feelings include being focused, positive, satisfied, flexible, good-humored and confident. The Achievement motivation is based on the need for success, mastery and aggression which gives rise to feelings of, or rejoicing in, success – hence the term "clappy".

ZAPPY employees are the opposite of mad. Feeling zappy includes being disciplined, responsible, committed, challenged or inspired, enacting altruism, and having a sense of higher meaning. The Actualisation motivation is being met and is based on the need for knowledge, meaning, spirituality and creativity that promotes a sense of purpose or elation, hence the term "zappy".

I thought that converting the opposite ends of the boredom–motivation continuum into fun names (i.e. from sad to happy, from bad to clappy, from mad to zappy) might help some people to avoid the denial and shame that seems to accompany discussions of boredom. I also think these terms are useful in presentations, where memorable terminology wins attention.

For my part I'm perfectly prepared to admit to boredom, frustration or alienation. For me, but perhaps not for others, recognizing the suppression of my needs by taking note of the experience of boredom symptoms is the most direct route to fixing the problem of personal motivation.

CHAPTER 5: AN IDEA WHOSE TIME HAD COME

History of ideas

IN THE HISTORY OF IDEAS, similar new concepts seem to emerge in parallel, even when different proponents have never met or interacted. The most famous example is probably the naturalists Charles Darwin and Alfred Russel Wallace separately reaching similar conclusions about evolution through natural selection (after learning of each other's work, they jointly presented papers about it, in 1858).

This phenomenon seems to suggest that big insights occur when the time is ripe. In the same way, the emergence of a needs-based approach to motivation is claimed by a number of authors in recent years. It's a theory whose time has come.

As I've already made clear, my early study and research interests up to 1989 were bedeviled by opposition from the dominant theories of the cognitive and behavioral psychologists. My final landing place was within the movement proposed by the humanist and needs-based theorists promoting intrinsic motivation. They hold that human behaviors are motivated by the desire to fulfill a human need – in other words, that our actions are the result of often hidden internal drives, needs or innate instincts.

Specifically, in the field of employee or workplace motivation, there are now a number of champions of needs based motivation. Some are more speculative than others and some are more persuasive than others. Below I introduce some of the better-known theorists and their take on intrinsic or needs-based motivation. I'm doing little more than touching on their models to demonstrate their central conclusions. I'm not attempting critique, explanation or analysis.

Champions of motivation

Sigmund Freud (1925): human drives and animal instincts

Freud suggested that human motivation was derived from the two basic animal instincts for procreation and for survival. This explained the human experience of sex and aggression (or love and war). Freud maintained that these basic animal instincts were modified in humans by means of the civilising influences of education and culture. However, he claimed that the highest human creative achievements are an expression of the synthesis of the sexual and aggressive instincts.

Abraham Maslow (1943): five drives in order

US-based psychologist Maslow published a paper in 1943 called *A Theory of Human Motivation*, in which he said that people had five sets of needs, which come in a strict order. He was subject to the attitudes of the times which held that, as an outcome of education and development, some humans operate on a higher plane than others: hence his hierarchy of needs. As each level of needs is satisfied, the desire to fulfil the next set kicks in. The well-known model below is an interpretation of Maslow's hierarchy of needs represented as a pyramid, with the more basic needs at the bottom.

Figure: Maslow's hierarchy of needs

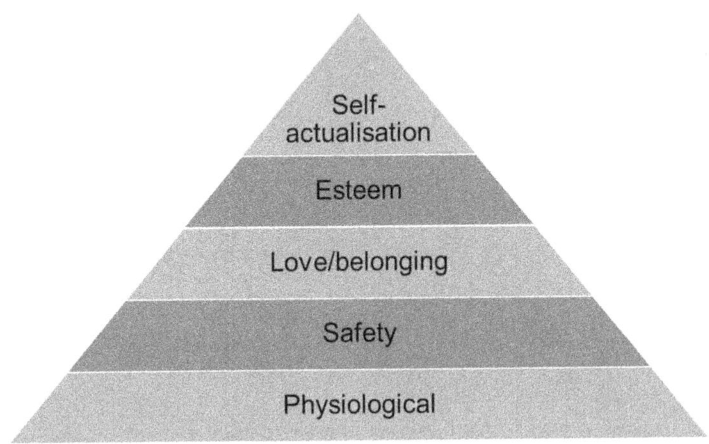

Despite its lack of empirical evidence and furphy that only two per cent of humans reach self-actualisation, Maslow's theory has been widely adopted by business management theorists. It struck a chord with 20th century managers and is still used in in management and business training today, probably because it rejects the simplistic reward-and-punishment model. It points to the universal truth of intrinsic motivation – capturing the hearts and minds of employees.

Frederick Herzberg (1959): two factor theory

Herzberg's hygiene and motivator (satisfier) factors theory is another widely referenced and popular idea in the business world. Herzberg suggests that there are a set of hygiene factors necessary to staying in a job, and a set of motivators that determine long-term employee motivation and performance. Business leaders seem to favour this theory because it combines extrinsic motivators such as pay and intrinsic motivations.

David McClelland (1961): acquired needs theory

McClelland's book *The Achieving Society* brought to public attention his theory of acquired needs. It found widespread support in the business world. According to the theory, individuals acquire three types of needs as a result of their life experiences: the need for Achievement, or to excel (nACH); for Affiliation, or to relate (nAFF); and to have Authority/Power, or influence others (nPOW). McClelland asserts that all individuals possess a combination of these needs, which can be demonstrated by empirical research.

Clayton P. Alderfer (1972): ERG theory

In 1972, American psychologist Alderfer tried to align Maslow's hierarchy with more recent empirical studies. He reshuffled the needs into a reduced set of three, which he called Existence, Relatedness and Growth, giving rise to acronym ERG, and the label ERG Theory. It holds that if we are unable to satisfy any one need, we put more effort into satisfying the others.

Rosabeth Moss Kanter (2001): Evolve!

Harvard Business School Professor Moss Kanter's 2001 book was ostensibly about succeeding in the digital age, but her approach to management and staffing is unmistakably needs-based. She posits that employee commitment relies on how well organisations can make connections with our skills and information processing. People have cognitive, emotional and moral skills and we therefore process information, rationally, emotionally and spiritually/morally. Organisations can offer three types of information processing as the basis for commitment – Mastery, Membership and Meaning.

Paul R. Lawrence & Nitin Nohria (2002): Driven

American organisational psychologists Lawrence and Nohria were much acclaimed for their book about how human nature shapes our choices. They say that four basic drives have evolved over time via the impact of civilisation, and are important in the dynamics and success of organisations. Each drive has both positive and negative expressions.

The four drives are:

- To Acquire: objects and experiences that improve our status relative to others (the basis of ambition and competition but also of the negative envy)
- To Bond: establish long term bonds with others based on reciprocity (the basis of caring, loyalty and social relationships but also of the division of "us and them")
- To Learn: about and make sense of our world, which is largely our own social creation (the basis of curiosity, problem solving, knowledge, skills but also of the negative self-destruction)
- To Defend: ourselves, our families and friends, our beliefs and our resources (the basis of individual, collective reactive responses but also of the negative war).

Only the first three are innate drives. The fourth is a reactive source of energy and requires an external threat.

Daniel Pink (2009): Drive

Pink's book was successful in bringing the intrinsic drive and needs theories to the attention of a wider, popular business audience. He gathered his ideas from needs theorists to create a model of motivation with three elements: Autonomy – the drive to direct our own lives; Mastery – the drive to get better at something that matters; and Purpose – the drive to do service for something larger than ourselves. Pink's major point is referencing Edward Deci's work (see below), demonstrating that in fact rewards can undermine rather than promote motivation. He has hit a chord and is widely published. Although he has three drives with different names, they all appear to be a variation of a single drive for autonomy, purpose or meaning.

Edward L. Deci (1975): intrinsic motivation

It is always difficult to compare and contrast interpretations of drives-based motivation. However, for me, one authority stands out. Since the 1995 publication of his book *Why we do what we do*, Deci, a professor at the University of Rochester, New York, has been promoting drives and has gone further by suggesting that the need for autonomy or freedom is the key to motivation. He also asserts that this need is dependent upon autonomy supporting external conditions. He offers a similar story to my Eureka moment, which pointed me to the suppression of verbalisation as a cause of boredom. In *Why we do what we do* (at page 109) Deci wrote:

“One of the things that has amazed me about the hundreds of bright accomplished college students I’ve known through the years is how many of them have told me they don’t express their real feelings and beliefs. If they did they say, they would feel selfish and guilty, and people wouldn’t like them. They can’t be who they really are because of fear or shame.”

Here we have echoes of the descriptions of boredom and the underlying distaste and dislike, even denial, of the condition. When a need is aroused but has to be denied or suppressed, there are feelings of shame or frustration.

For Deci, freedom – or his preferred term “autonomy” – is the supportive environment for motivation. But he emphasizes that “autonomy supporting environment” is not permissiveness. For him autonomy support is hard work and requires being clear, being consistent and setting limits. Again we have an echo of the Polish film about the Easter decorations. In other words, the freedom within structure that I discovered in my Capita research a few years earlier – but failed to publicise.

In 2000, Deci collaborated with his fellow University of Rochester professor Richard Ryan to follow up Deci's earlier speculations about needs-based intrinsic motivation. The results of their empirical experiments to demonstrate the interplay of extrinsic and intrinsic motivation was published in *Psychological Inquiry* ("The 'what' and 'why' of goal pursuits: Human needs and the self-determination of behaviour") and *American Psychologist* ("Self-determination theory and the facilitation of intrinsic motivation, social development, and well-being"). Their most valuable breakthrough was the first, which provided a model of intrinsic motivation as the satisfaction of three basic needs namely:

Relatedness – to interact, be connected to and caring for others

Competence – to seek to control the outcome and experience mastery

Autonomy – to be in control of one's own life and act in harmony with one's integrated self

According to Deci and Ryan, the supportive conditions that ensure the satisfaction of intrinsic needs is freedom, choice and autonomy. Thus managers and leaders should look to support autonomy amongst their employees.

Ascent of needs-based motivation

Edward Deci and I, both with strong Freudian traditions, are not far apart in our thinking. Probably the only difference is a matter of semantics.

- My term Affiliation is close to Deci's Relatedness
- My term Achievement is close to Deci's Competence
- My term Actualisation is close to Deci's Autonomy

The major difference is my addition of the dimension of boredom with its apathy, frustration and alienation as symptoms of motivation denied. Deci knew about these experiences and relates many in his book (Why we do what we do, 1995) but has not put them into a structure or continuum of experiences and symptoms that move between motivation needs expressed or permitted and motivation needs suppressed or denied.

Deci also claims less for the third drive by naming it Autonomy (freedom). I hold that Actualisation includes spirituality, creativeness and vocation. For me, the claim for something higher, something special or bigger than ourselves, is essential. Artists often speak of the something else that inspires them: "it came to me", the "spirit moved me". It is this supra-human dimension that uses individuals as a vessel or means to end that I am trying to capture, whatever one calls it: being in the zone, or going with the flow.

This last and apparently strongest need or force or source of energy is the most difficult to describe, yet the easiest to recognise. It is the urge for something bigger than ourselves, the need to express what really matters. For this we need appropriate freedom. Think of what prize-winning authors or painters so often say upon accepting their award: "Now I can afford to do what I love full time." However, we must also remember that creative people often set themselves a daily schedule that controls and structures their work. As one author told me: "I start writing at 9 and end at 12, then edit for the rest of the day."

Whatever the characteristics attributed to the third need, it's becoming widely accepted that we all share the three: the more obvious ones of companionship and individual achievement and the more obscure one of higher attainment. All leaders and organisations that want the best from their employees or members need to remember how important it is to establish the correct balance between freedom and structure, and between autonomy and control.

All types of boredom offer a sign that a motivation or a need for self-expression is being blocked. The blockage can be *exogenous* – something from the external world preventing an employee from satisfying their need or expressing their drive and impulses. Or, in cases of sometimes chronic boredom, it can be *endogenous* – being blocked by individuals themselves. They may be forcing themselves to always keep quiet or to be inactive because they either fear reprimand or are determined to be polite.

It may be that individuals move between these three conditions, experiencing the domination and denial of different drives at different times. But every individual is motivated by all three drives and responds to them in different ways. Every individual in the workplace has the need for love, the need for achievement and the need for meaning. But at any one time, the three needs are unlikely to be playing an equal role in terms of emotions, thoughts, opinions, behaviours and motivation.

Fuzzy logic

Strictly, fuzzy logic is a mathematical concept, introduced by Professor Lotfi Zadeh of the University of California, Berkeley in the 1960s. However, the concept has been applied more widely. Some years ago, I became interested by his writings about fuzzy logic, in which he asserts that our brains are capable of spontaneous recognition of groups of things that share the same characteristics. For instance, without specifically being taught, our brain will recognise a member of the bird family, even if it looks different to the birds we already know. Our brain, given a choice of objects, will correctly identify the one that belongs to a range of other similar but not identical groups. Again our brain will identify the object that does not belong to the group.

During my consulting days I ran workshops for human resources professionals that explored the topic of employee motivation. These workshops confirmed that people unwittingly recognised the three types of needs underpinning their motivation. Their fuzzy logic correctly identified three types of needs.

I would ask the workshop group the question: "What do you feel, do or say when you are feeling bored at work? Try to remember the last time you felt bored. Write down each behaviour or feeling on a separate sticky note".

While participants thought and wrote, I'd draw three columns on the white board headed "sleepy", "angry" and "escape", which represent the symptoms of boredom that result from repression or suppression of the three motivation drives (i.e. Affiliation, Achievement and Actualisation). Without giving any explanation of the tripartite model of boredom, I then asked participants to place their behaviours or feelings under the appropriate heading.

Invariably, over 90 per cent of people placed their notes under the right heading – they instinctively, by means of fuzzy logic, recognised which of their feelings or behaviours belonged to which group or category.

I then asked participants to identify which of the three types of boredom best represented their most recent experience, and thus each named which of the three motivation drives was currently being blocked, suppressed or thwarted in their own case. We'd then discuss the insight in the context of understanding the participant's current needs, and think about ways to take action to express those needs, make decisions about work and guide their future career.

For example, one participant identified Actualisation boredom and recognised that his need for meaning and creativity was not being met. Another participant recognised Affiliate boredom, which meant that she was craving more bonding, teamwork and socialisation.

These experiences reflected a moment in time. Each individual may have had different motivational challenge at another time, or in another set of circumstances or another workplace. The thing is, without guidance or prompting, people instinctively recognised the underlying cause of their motivational blockage.

CHAPTER SIX: FREEDOM WITH STRUCTURE

From students to employees

THE WORLD OF WORK has been the focus of my investigations during my decades as a consultant and it's the area in which I'm both most confident and have a proven track record. Indeed, the consultancy I established in 1989, Hinds Research (previously Hinds Workforce Research) endures to this day, with its modern digital incarnation:

Peoplepie Surveys (www.peoplepie.com) Although I began in the field of education exploring the nature and drivers of student motivation, it became obvious that the world of work and the workplace offered greater research opportunities and a more positive reception.

In terms of opportunities, Australian government rules made it difficult to access more than a few hundred students at a time to act as research subjects. By contrast, as a human resources manager or consultant, I was able to access a few thousand employees for each and every project – and was paid to do so!

In terms of reception, it seems strange, but teachers appeared lukewarm to the findings of my early educational research. I well remember a presentation to teachers at a senior girl's school given by way of a "thank you" for letting me access their students. They were interested but basically felt that the results were not a surprise to them "I always knew that" was a typical response.

Whilst the teacher response might have been low-key, the leaders of organisations that actively sponsored customised research to measure and to identify the drivers of their employee motivation took the results seriously enough to act upon them. Throughout the decades, evidence was increasingly available and disseminated that higher employee motivation means higher performance, sales and profits; not to mention harmony, change-readiness and loyalty.

Today there are numerous authoritative studies, papers and books confirming the positive impacts of employee motivation on such outcomes as staff turnover, retention, customer service, innovation, safety, culture change and shareholder value (Kular, 2008). Today, most successful organisations in both public and private sector conduct employee opinion surveys focused on employee motivation (variously called by other names such as satisfaction, engagement or well-being). In 2010, the government of Great Britain, responding to the McCloud Report, posited the promotion of employee engagement and motivation as the focus of all government policy, programs and investment.

I was fortunate to begin my journey in the field of education (to which I later returned) as it gave me ample opportunity to recognize the importance of student boredom as a key to unlocking an insight into the dynamics of both boredom and motivation. As covered in previous chapters, in the early 1980s and using student research, I was able to develop my Eureka speculation that motivation can turn into boredom, that motivation operates on a continuum with boredom and that it responds to both monotony and repression of verbal expression. Moving from education to the corporate world, I conducted my primary PhD research at a large financial services company and my hypothesis was confirmed, giving it the status of a theory (see "Unleashing the giant" in Chapter One). An unexpected outcome of the research was the identification of three rather than two clusters of symptoms of boredom/motivation, demonstrating the expression or existence of three rather than two human needs or instincts. This led to my 1995 book *The Hinds model of company success* in which I outlined my theory or model of employee motivation and boredom.

NEED		MOTIVATION	BOREDOM
Affiliation	We	From Interest	To Apathy
Achievement	Me	From Satisfaction	To Frustration
Actualisation	It	From Commitment	To Alienation

In this book so far I've only briefly mentioned my consulting research objectives to identify the most potent causes or drivers of employee motivation/boredom. Now it's time to share with you the results of that work.

Reporting motivation

Motivation can be reported with either a single aggregated motivation score or as a set of three scores, one each for Affiliation, Achievement and Actualisation. Over the years we've reported to consultancy clients using both methods, and in doing so have found the single score more practical and effective for workplace surveying.

This is because it helps keep employees and their managers focused on the drivers where action needs to occur (leading indicators) rather than on the motivation outcome (lagging indicators).

Debating the impact of subtle differences in the tripartite motivation elements is not as helpful to work teams as it is to debate which drivers to take action on and how.

When individuals want to understand their personal motivation, an appreciation of the three needs and whether or not they are being satisfied, can be extremely helpful. However, for work teams, it is the workplace drivers that have the most powerful impact on whether the three needs are being met and hence on total motivation scores. So that is where we want attention focused when surveyed teams receive their results.

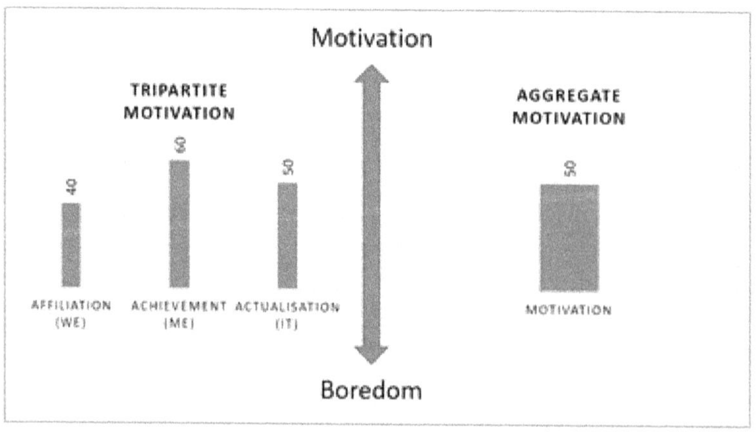

The secret to motivating employees

In the early 1980s, anecdotal literature offered many – and growing – suggestions for the influencers or drivers of employee motivation. But business literature tended towards the view that the causes of employee motivation fell mainly into three areas:

- Employee reward or recognition (usually financial)
- Job characteristics or design (including performance objectives)
- Behaviours or style of the immediate manager.

In the years since, there's been extensive 'solutions' literature offering a diverse range of drivers based on research or experience. Indeed, offering quick and easy solutions to engage and motivate employees or to achieve change has guaranteed the sales success of a number of business/personal development publications. Especially those with snappy titles, we note Kenneth Blanchard and Spencer Johnson's *The One Minute Manager* (1982), Johnson's *Who Moved My Cheese?* (1998), or John Kotter and Holger Rathgeber's *Our Iceberg is Melting* (2005).

Back when I started my research, it was apparent that there might well be a more complex range of employee motivation/boredom drivers, so I stretched my research parameters widely. For my 1990, Capita research survey described in an earlier chapter, my background investigation incorporated all the available literature offering the causes of boredom and of motivation, and also included the anecdotal evidence offered by employees in the focus groups I'd conducted. As a result, I gathered 522 questions or statement items which were eventually included in the foundation employee survey. Of these, 437 measured for the antecedents, contributors or drivers of motivation/boredom.

The subsequent statistical analysis of those 437 items against employee motivation levels identified 44 items or issues that were deemed to be extremely strong or potent motivation drivers. Another term for strong drivers is 'statistically significant'. (see *The science of analysis* at the end of this chapter). However, further statistical analysis offered that these 44 potent drivers of employee motivation actually distributed into two main groups, which I named culture and manager.

Culture Driver: included issues such as support, quality over quantity work, respect, social exchange, clear lines of communication, bureaucracy, concern, teamwork, value, communication, open-expression, information about strategy and objectives, channels for input, development opportunities, training, reward, recognition, cohesive systems, and regular performance reviews.

Manager Driver: included issues such as provision of autonomy, support of achievement, openness, courtesy, understanding, warmth, promotion of confidence and talent, verbal recognition, honest two-way communication, inviting discussion or criticism, providing feedback, recognition of job worth, objectivity and fairness, performance development, and having good planning and management skills.

Look carefully at the two sets of drivers of employee motivation. Within each set, the issues actually fall into two types. One type describes what Edward Deci (1995) calls autonomy, or freedom. For example, from Culture we have respect, open expression and channels for input, and from Manager we find openness and inviting discussion or criticism. A second type is what Deci calls autonomy supporting systems or limitations. For example, in Culture we find clear lines of communication and cohesive systems, and from Manager we find providing feedback and planning.

A few years before Deci published his insights, my Capita research produced an unexpected result: statistically, issues group together in a way that integrates freedoms with freedom-supporting measures or systems. Of course freedom can become permissiveness, and systems can become authoritarian controls. Neither promote motivation but instead enforce boredom, anger and alienation. However, it is freedom *within* structure that is the secret to employee motivation – indeed, to all human motivation.

One of the newer features of these drivers was the importance of an open culture characterized by clear and honest information, combined with the freedom for employees to ask questions and express their opinions, even if negative. Leaders of the day seemed to be afraid of allowing negative feedback from their employees. The reasoning was that employees needed to be protected from negative opinions they might otherwise not have shared or even thought of. This irrational or fearful leadership response simply resulted in silent employee cohorts, which denied leaders the opportunity to benefit from their employees' experience, knowledge or innovation. Today leadership more willingly seeks employee opinion and feedback, both negative and positive – a wise development.

Just as society changes, so does the nature of work and relationships between employees and employers, and since my initial investigation, my further studies and Hinds Research consultancy projects have provided an evolving picture of employee motivation. The ongoing results have supplied new motivation drivers, reallocated known drivers into different groups or factors, and validated a driver's known strength on employee motivation.

We have implemented surveys for over 100 Australian and international organisations from both the public and private sectors: ranging between 1,000 and 35,000 employees. The organisations operate in a wide range of fields, including technology, telecommunications, logistics, manufacturing, professional and legal services, post, insurance, banking and uniformed services such as customs, police and defense. We've used employee focus groups to probe for new, emerging drivers of motivation, over time adding new and better drivers whilst discarding those that have lost potency.

All the more recent results and findings have not altered our early important insight: that motivation and its intrinsic needs best find their expression in an environment that provides autonomy or freedom within agreed constraints or a confidence-building structure. One without the other does not work. They are the Tweedledum and Tweedledee of motivation in the organizational Wonderland (with apologies to Lewis Carroll).

Freedom comes with agreed limitations, autonomy comes within safety guidelines, and creativity comes with disciplines.

We finally established a firm and sustained set of seven driver groups. These seven drivers with their five sub-elements were not randomly chosen but identified using rigorous scientific processes, methods, disciplines and analyses (as discussed in the side bar). Of immense significance is that we can see that each driver integrates items that represent freedoms together with items that represent useful and confidence building systems or controls. The secret of motivating employees remains the same whichever aspect of the working environment you look at: freedom integrated within structure. The combination of freedom with structure is reflected in the short definitions of each driver group, which are more fully discussed in the next chapter. The seven drivers of employee motivation are:

1. **JOB:** Use of my skills and energy within a worthwhile balanced role
2. **EMPLOYER:** Concern and collaboration within an admired company
3. **INFLUENCE:** Open opinions and respect within a planned order
4. **DEVELOPMENT:** Training and recognition within a fair system
5. **ALIGNMENT:** Empowerment and autonomy within an agreed strategy
6. **LEADERSHIP:** Communication and honesty within strong effectiveness
7. **MANAGER:** Support and openness within effective management behaviours.

The listed order of the drivers reflects the order of statistical strength.

Whilst all driver groups are significantly strong enough to make a difference to motivation levels, there is a tendency for some to be stronger than others as reflected in list numbering shown here.

In terms of the results of an employee survey, action must be taken on the lowest scoring driver – the lowest hanging fruit. Now having identified the seven most potent drivers of motivation, I was able to add a causative framework to my tripartite model of motivation.

Figure: The seven drivers of employee motivation

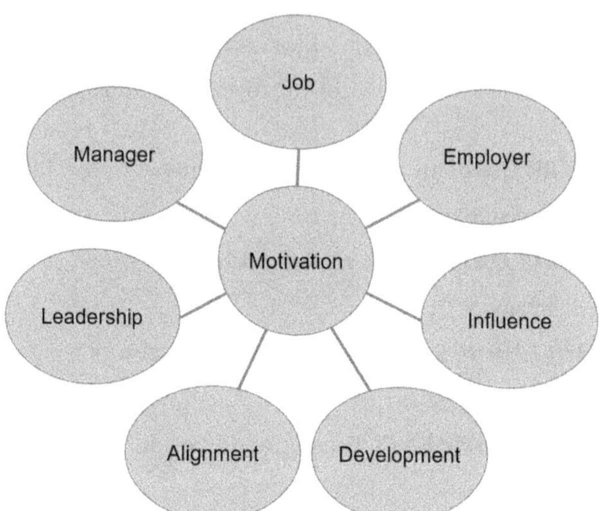

Many companies have measured motivation and its drivers using our survey called the Employee Motivation and Performance Index or EMPI®.

Each team, business unit, function or location received its own set of EMPI® results. The results were used by leaders and managers to guide actions that delivered positive and profitable outcomes.

An updated version of our survey designed specifically for teams is accessible today via Peoplepie Surveys. (www.peoplepie.com)

Over the years, we were able to gather information about the positive outcomes that raising employee motivation actually delivered. Depending on the issues that were of concern, outcomes included reduction of turnover, increase of sales, improved customer service and reduction in processing times - as outlined in our case studies. However, more significant were the issues that bedeviled a company that gained clarity from the special analysis of the responses to an employee motivation survey. Let me give you a simple, real-life example of how statistical analysis works to clarify issues and assumptions.

A client of ours asked us to use a survey project to help them to make a decision about their staff. One half of the staff were in uniform, in line with their safety and protection role, while the other half were not in uniform in line with their support and administrative role. According to leadership, there was a great deal of background noise, made louder by the staff union, asking for new uniforms and the extension of the uniform policy to those staff in support. A great deal of management time was being expended on this topic in meetings, where it was claimed that it would make a profound difference to staff morale and motivation. The problem was that new uniforms and a greater number of staff in uniforms meant expenditure of millions of dollars. The client wanted to know: would this expenditure deliver performance benefits?

There was a second problem. Their uniformed team members were not completing their weekly reports, which were needed by managers and team leaders. Over the years, no amount of training or supervision was able to increase the fulfillment of this essential task.

Taking the last problem first, the survey design included a special set of skill-testing items to measure for skill levels on a self- assessment basis. Subsequent factor analysis of the survey responses to these items showed that “report writing” did not group with other team-member capabilities required for their safety and protection role. “Report writing” fell into the skill group expected of a manager, such as planning and organization. No amount of hassling was going to change report writing from a natural skill for managers to a natural one for team members. As a result of our findings, leadership implemented a solution whereby reports were completed by managers based on a tick and check form from team members. Everyone was happy!

Now back to the uniform issue. Survey results confirmed that 80% of uniformed staff wanted a new uniform. But correlation analysis of the responses to the survey demonstrated that despite this desire, new uniforms would have no impact on the motivation, loyalty or performance of staff. Again the results showed that about 50% of non-uniformed staff wanted uniforms, but correlation analysis demonstrated that it would make no actual difference to motivation levels. The issue of uniforms was not a motivation-enhancing one. New or extra uniforms were "nice to have" not an organisational "have to have". Leadership decided to not spend the millions of dollars required.

Using statistics to confirm seven drivers

Let's now look more closely at the statistical evidence underpinning the operation of the seven drivers of motivation defined and offered in this book. Based on our most recent employee survey results, our analysis first identified the most motivating items in a particular workplace. These were then statistically clustered to identify common factors. Each resultant group of motivators was in turn correlated against employee motivation/boredom. The strongest or most potent groups were selected and named and reduced to a selection of the five strongest items each. In other words: find motivating items, find out how they group and pick those that are more strongly motivating, discarding weaker items beyond five.

The following table below lists the seven workplace driver groups ranked in descending order of their correlation coefficient against (i.e. strength of impact on) employee motivation. Anything above 0.30 is deemed to be a very strong correlation coefficient, indicating a strong driver of employee motivation. The drivers generally hold good across a variety of employee populations, organisations or countries.

Motivation driver	Average strength of correlation with motivation
Job	0.59
Employer	0.53
Influence	0.51
Development	0.48
Alignment	0.48
Leadership	0.43
Manager	0.37

The variable strength between drivers shows the greater importance of the Job, Employer and Influence driver groups. This contrasts with many business world assumptions that Leadership and Manager are the most important drivers of employee motivation. Leadership and Manager training and mentoring are the more typical focus of investment and yet may not be the most valuable.

The performance score on the driver group, not the correlation scores, determines where to take action. The correlations are only of interest to the researcher in confirming that the driver group has a high chance of making an impact on employee motivation. The actual scores are what the manager uses to determine action priorities.

In the following chart of average drivers and motivation scores from surveys of 134,380 employees we see that in our database Influence and Leadership are the lowest scoring drivers and therefore most often requiring attention.

Chart: Average driver and motivation scores

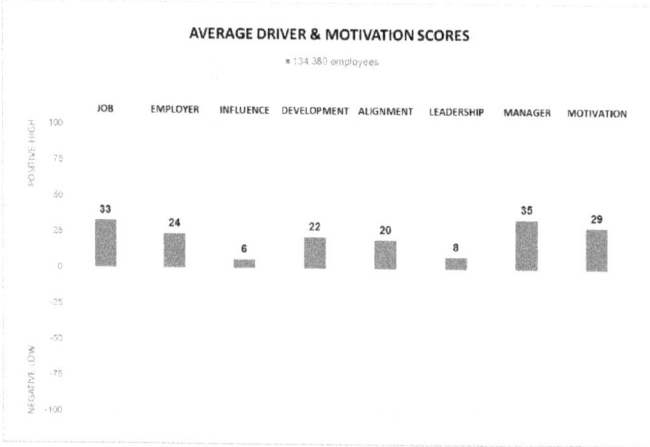

In the next chart, we see the wide range of scores that can occur in small groups or teams, ranges which are hidden in the results of the larger organisation.

Chart: Driver and motivation score in teams of 5 > 15 people

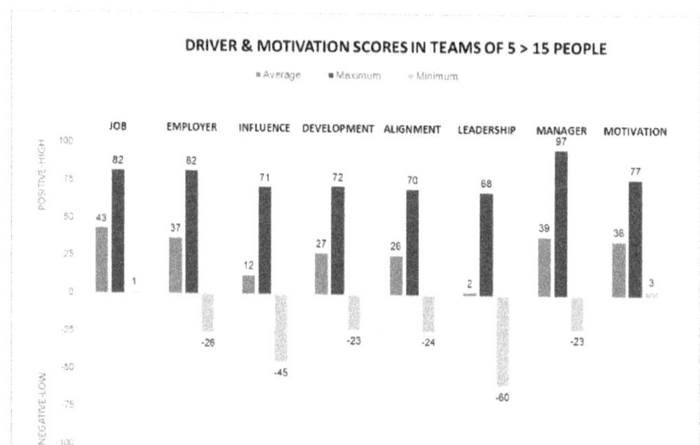

A high driver score means that the issues are driving motivation up, but a low or even negative score means that they are driving motivation down and, in the case of negative scores, may well be causing employee boredom, apathy, frustration and alienation. When this occurs, serious business problems arise. It becomes more difficult to attract and keep talent, reduce absenteeism, achieve change strategies, win sales and maintain quality customer service. Some companies can be in danger of more serious problems such as industrial sabotage and lack of business trust or loyalty.

The importance of the seven drivers in having a significant impact on employee motivation was confirmed in all of our subsequent client research projects. Repetition of the research confirmed the seven driver framework and ensured we delivered accurate and trustworthy results for managers and leaders.

This means that the efforts and actions that managers take in response to the survey results is not wasted and employees are not misled. The results from these surveys are trustworthy for three main reasons:

- the measure of employee motivation used is accurate and complete,
- the identification of the true motivation drivers is reliable, and
- only the strongest or most potent driver groups are retained.

My faith in our survey's reliability meant that my colleagues and I were able to say to clients that if they took action on the lowest scoring drivers, we would guarantee their employee motivation would rise. "Hand on heart, money-back guarantee!'

In over 20 years consulting we have never had to return a fee.

The science of analysis

In this chapter I make reference to scientific rigor based on statistical analysis. Some readers will be quite happy to accept statements about statistical grouping, strength of drivers and impact potency without requiring further explanation. However, many will quite correctly demand that I give further explanation of the bases of my assertions, especially as they offer information you may wish to use or rely on. So this section is for the scientifically minded and the skeptical. If you're more interested in moving on to simply understanding the workplace drivers, skip to the next chapters.

As described in the section called 'Unleashing the giant', the questionnaire in my initial investigative survey was designed in an unusual way and set the pattern for all subsequent projects. All the questions were constructed in the form of statements requiring a response on a five point scale ranging from strongly agree to strongly disagree: offered as YES, yes, ?, no, NO. This is known as a modified Likert scale and is often favored by researchers. It is easy for participants to answer and helps to support the very high response rate (over 85%) that is necessary if one is going to use the results for advanced statistical analysis.

In the initial Capita survey, statements were designed to test for causes of motivation/boredom and for symptoms of boredom. Statistical analysis of employee responses allowed me to factor or cluster items to create groups of items that are significantly similar to each other, that are describing the same thing. This method was used to identify the three factors of motivation/boredom symptoms as well as the workplace motivation driving factors Culture and Manager.

The term "significant" means that something occurs more frequently than by chance or luck. It may be luck that it rains when there is a cloud in the sky, but it is significant if it rains nearly every time there is a cloud in the sky. So the use of the word significant means a very strong likelihood that when one thing occurs, another thing occurs.

Our survey data was used to analyse relationships between items tested as drivers of motivation and items used to test motivation itself.

Multi-variate correlation analyses were used to identify significant relationships.

However as many will already know, correlation alone does not prove causation. Proving causation can be achieved in two ways. Firstly, with statistical correlation within a valid model of cause and effect and secondly, by using statistical correlation and evidence that the linked relationships hold true when measured repeatedly over time. This is called longitudinal tracking.

The surveys were built around an academically demonstrated model of cause and effect as described earlier with evidence from personal experience, extensive literature and focus group descriptions of motivation/boredom antecedents.

In addition, the process Hinds Research used and repeated with all employee and culture research projects was to use statistical grouping of issues (items), supported by correlation analysis to determine the presence of a relationship with longitudinal tracking to prove causation. This methodology allowed us to constantly update and refine our understanding of the symptoms and nature of motivation/boredom and its three needs.

As our research continued over the years we were able to incorporate emerging issues of the workplace ecosystem and reflect correctly modern drivers of employee motivation and engagement. These included changing conditions like the emergence of Generation X; teamwork, leadership, renewed interest in bullying and discrimination; differences between geographical or cultural regions; and differences between public and private sector organisations, ensuring that our survey tools delivered ongoing accuracy and reliability.

In conclusion, statistical analysis of survey responses identifies items that are significantly "like each other" and hence identify a common group that may not be immediately obvious. It can demonstrate where one item (or group of items) is likely to precede another item (or group of items) hence showing cause and effect i.e. if this happens then that is highly likely to happen. Analysis is very useful in confirming or rejecting speculation. However, it is always best to begin with a well-argued theory, model and credible assumptions to avoid error in reaching conclusions.

CHAPTER 7: THE DRIVERS OF MOTIVATION

Engagement or motivation?

STUDENTS OF BUSINESS and even those familiar with the world of business and employment tend to use the term "employee engagement" instead of "employee motivation". Influenced by Freud, the early organisational writers Abraham Maslow and Frederick Herzberg used the labels motivation and motivators. In his seminal book *Why we do what we do*, Edward Deci promoted intrinsic motivation versus the then more popular extrinsic motivation (e.g. rewards and reviews). He used the term motivation exclusively: it's referenced in the index at least 35 times. However, over time the term employee motivation has been overtaken by the now more widely use term of employee engagement. There have been other popular terms such as job satisfaction, employee commitment or involvement, but almost universally the accepted term today appears to be engagement.

The McCloud Report (2009) definition holds that: "Employee engagement is a workplace designed to ensure that employees are committed to their organisation's goals and values, motivated to contribute to organisational success and are able at the same time to enhance their own sense of well-being." Using this report, the UK government set a goal to increase employee engagement as a major government priority and backed it with funding. This decision was triggered by national organisational surveys that showed that the UK is ranked ninth in employee engagement levels amongst the largest economies. Both national and business leaders accept the evidence that increasing employee engagement levels has a knock-on effect of raising performance, profitability and profitability.

The problem with the term motivation in management discourse appears to be its lack of connection to business objectives. By contrast, leaders might feel more comfortable with the terms engagement and commitment as there is an implied 'with what' or 'to what?' query, which in turn suggests the answer 'to this organisation'. Motivation on the other hand does not specifically assume a business-friendly objective. Motivation is an energy source that only flows if there is an object, but that object may be far from the business world. Hence today management language tends to use employee engagement – with its additional connotation of motivation directed towards the service of the employer.

Evidence demonstrates emphatically that the business benefits claimed for employee engagement also hold for employee motivation. Higher motivation leads to higher performance, reduced turnover, higher sales and higher stability and sustainability. The narrower meaning of engagement puts the concept in a strait jacket of subordination to the commercial and mercantile objectives, whereas motivation reintroduces humanity, clarifies its cluster of feelings and behaviours and allows us to visualise its opposition to the experience of boredom. For this reason, I have stuck with the term motivation in this book.

The proof is in the pudding

Having created a survey based testing instrument designed to identify the appropriate action or the best solution to employee motivation levels or issues, it was important to confirm or modify it in the light of longitudinal (long-term) experience. Repeating our survey many times in different companies with similar outcomes provided us with the necessary proof of value. I needed to demonstrate that the survey information about driver performance provided managers and leaders with insights, advice and a set of practical actions that *always* improved the motivation of their team or organisation.

Thus it was that in the initial years of development, my employee motivation and drivers' survey required verification in the real world of business or organisations. It was all very well to have demonstrated statistically that drivers theoretically made a difference to employee motivation. But in the real world, if managers took action on their drivers, would employee motivation rise? It was therefore critical to gather clients who would want to run the survey – then called The Employee Motivation and Performance Index (or EMPI®) – and share with me their views on its benefits and effectiveness.

If proof is in the pudding, then I was looking for some puddings! It was with some dismay that I engaged with my first major client. It was not an old fashioned traditional business, rather one of the new, advanced, computer technology companies and very successful at the time. Presenting to the senior executive team, I suggested that they might want to reduce employee boredom, raise employee motivation and achieve some of the contingent benefits such as loyalty and enhanced performance. "Nonsense," replied a loud voice from back of the room "We do not have a problem with employees who are bored. If they're bored – we sack them!"

This alerted me to the fact that, although I knew for certain that boredom is the opposite of motivation, the general public, and business people in particular, would neither accept nor countenance the possibility of bored employees. Even today, and with the new benefit of internet enabled access to literature, I've not been able to find much evidence that the scourge of boredom is in fact linked to the dynamics of motivation. Boredom is not readily recognised as the negative on the spectrum with the positive motivation. The reason remains that motivation is well studied, while boredom remains "a neglected topic" (Fisher 1993). It's almost as if it is invisible. It really only becomes visible when it occurs in individuals in extreme pathological forms and presents as a medical problem.

The few exceptions in academic literature appear to be brief references or long complex expositions from cognitive behaviourists. For example, according to Judy Willis (2014) "Neuroscience reveals that boredom hurts", whilst Sandi Mann (2014), UK based psychologists has evidence to suggest that "boring activities can result in increased creativity". Whilst she argues that boredom at work can be combatted by interesting work breaks, she gives only passing reference to the idea that tackling boredom is necessary if we are to retain skilled, motivated and healthy workers.

An even more ambitious piece by Schaufeli and Salanova (2014) fails to properly make the motivation/boredom continuum link. They provide a long discussion of burnout as a type of exhaustion, a brief reference to boredom as lack of stimulation and a lengthy consideration of engagement in which they assert it “is inversely related to burnout and boredom”.

So even today, it is best not to talk of employee boredom, but rather employee motivation or de-motivation. Boredom as a topic remains a “no-go” area. When I work with organisations and teams to take action on their results, my emphasis is on achieving employee motivation or raising employee motivation. It amounts to the same thing as reducing employee boredom. But by focusing on the positive – a preference in this age of positive psychology – I gain the support and involvement of leaders and managers.

So in gathering my puddings to demonstrate the truth and effectiveness of the EMPI® survey measures and results, I stopped making overt reference to boredom or bored employees. I should add that this overt abandonment of the “boredom” terminology came as a relief to both my consulting colleagues and my client organisations. Nevertheless, the basic science remains the same: the survey instrument contains the original measures of, and contributing factors to, both employee motivation *and* boredom.

Using the longitudinal validation of repeated surveys, the drivers of employee motivation measures were modified over time. As the world and society changes, so too do the conditions that support motivation. Much is made of changing age groups such as Generation X and different cultures under conditions of globalisation etc. We might speculate that a worker in Victorian England may have been more motivationally responsive to good pay and reasonable hours than today's employee, for whom such things may be part of the wallpaper. Thus the drivers or driver groups described below are the final version after over a decade of testing. However, it's surprising that over that period, most of the drivers are unchanged or have changed very little. This bears witness to the fact that human nature is slow to change, or very conservative or constant. We are not much different in our desires and needs from those of our forebears.

Incorporating the measures of the seven drivers within the survey meant that organisations and business units gained a base measure of their score on each driver and could use the scores to select priority actions. We'd advise them to focus on the one or two lowest scores, and not to charge at all drivers like a bull in a china shop. They would select and plan the action they would take. Where a low-scoring driver suggested action that was just plain impossible, we would advise them not to waste energy on it, but rather to move to the next lowest score, where they might have a better chance of success. This selection of the easier solution is what might be called "going through the open window when the front door is closed".

If a client took action to fix the areas identified by the low-scoring driver, we knew that the action on the low scoring driver was invariably followed by a motivation score improvement. Where low driver scores were translated into action implementation, the result was always a rise in employee motivation; sometimes within six months and certainly by the next annual survey. The reverse also proved to be true. Where organisations stopped taking driver-signaled action, employee motivation scores in the next survey would plateau as a warning. If lack of driver action continued, by the subsequent survey employee motivation would invariably drop, heralding its attendant ills such as higher turnover, higher accidents, and higher absenteeism. Actions on drivers were proved to be potent in all client case studies: happily, there were no exceptions.

Case study: A veritable leap year

When private sector or government organisations run employee surveys, they do so with the intention of fixing any people problems that are highlighted by the results. Some organisations succeed and others don't. This case study is the surprising instance of a government department which embraced their results and moved ahead in leaps and bounds in only one year.

You and I might normally argue that speed of responsiveness and ability to change would only occur in the private sector, in which case we'd be wrong. This case study proves it.

The government agency of nearly 3,000 people was led by a team of senior, experienced and thoughtful leaders. This leadership team genuinely wanted to use their employee survey to gather strategic information that would underpin an action strategy guided by data and analysis. Their willingness to be guided by data reflected the agency's purpose and composition as its role was to deliver key policy, analysis and information services to the community and other government agencies.

The organisation was staffed by highly skilled employees, many of whom possessed advanced postgraduate qualifications. The first survey results highlighted dramatic weaknesses in the Leadership and Influence drivers.

Primarily employees thought the leadership team were distant, uncommunicative and failing to operate as a unified team (i.e. the Leadership driver).

In addition, employees felt unable to participate in the work or operational planning, could not make their opinions heard and felt unappreciated or undervalued (i.e. the Influence driver). As a result, motivation across the entire agency was at an average of 34/100.

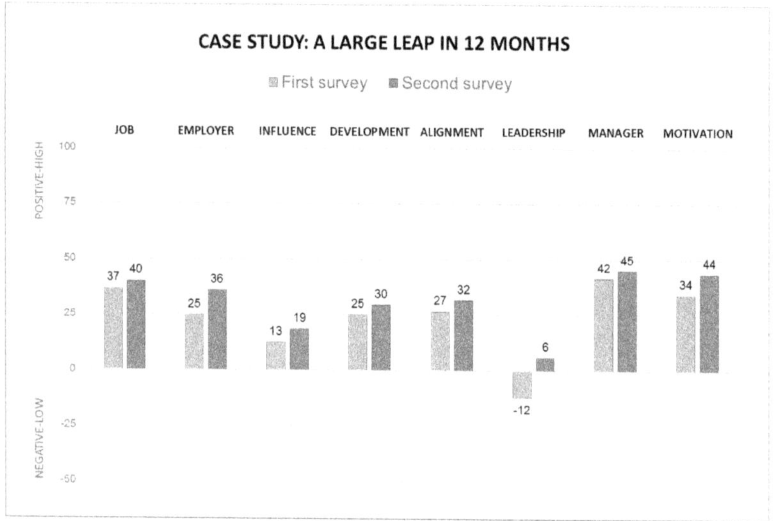

The leadership team were rather shocked by the findings but resolved to turn things around, and quickly. They spent two days as a team at an offsite conference to delve into the survey results and create action plan solutions that would directly address their weaker drivers. They bravely accepted that the negative score on the Leadership driver was their problem to fix and committed to repeat measurement within a year to make sure they acted swiftly.

Some of the actions they invested in were:

- disseminating the unedited survey results to employee teams, departments and divisions quickly via a manager led feedback program

- implementing four different interventions specifically designed to improve access and communications between leaders and employees

- refreshing the corporate plan and strategy with employee involvement via a cascading participation program
- regularly recrafting and sharing the key messages of the leadership team

What is important is that the actions were narrow in focus and targeted directly the two employee motivation drivers that the leaders wanted to 'fix'. And it worked.

Looking at the Second survey results there is a dramatic improvement on the two target drivers: Leadership went from negative 12 to positive 6, an improvement of 18 points. In addition, Influence also improved, moving from 13 to 19 points, an improvement of 6 points.

But what did this do to employee motivation? It leapt up. It moved from 34 to 44, a ten-point improvement which is an outstanding result to achieve within a single year. The motivation score increase was the direct result of improved performance on all seven motivation drivers. The tide was pushing in the right direction and employee motivation responded.

Our prediction has always been that action and improved scores on the drivers will always make a difference to scores on motivation. So witnessing the real life dynamic of drivers impacting on motivation so quickly was particularly gratifying. So presenting these results and congratulating this government agency on their success was one of the more rewarding consulting experiences.

Case study: That sinking feeling!

A slow leak that lets water into a boat is perilous. The boat will stay afloat for quite some time and then suddenly the pressure builds, the hole expands, and water flows in more quickly and the sinking of the boat speeds up.

I observed this phenomenon at close hand with one of my clients that was a large scale utility wholesaler. Over a period of four years their continued failure to take action on drivers delivered slow then more rapidly sinking motivation levels.

This company employed around 4,300 employees working in blue collar and white collar roles across a wide range of trades, skills and capabilities. The leadership team were comprised of people who had worked their way up from the line and professional managers and leaders brought in from other industries. The impetus to conduct an employee survey to understand motivation and culture was triggered by a thoughtful human resources executive who sadly departed the company before the four-year ongoing project began. Over the next four years the leadership team challenged, ignored and refuted the survey results. When warned that motivation and job performance would begin to deteriorate unless actions were taken, these warnings were ignored or indeed rejected.

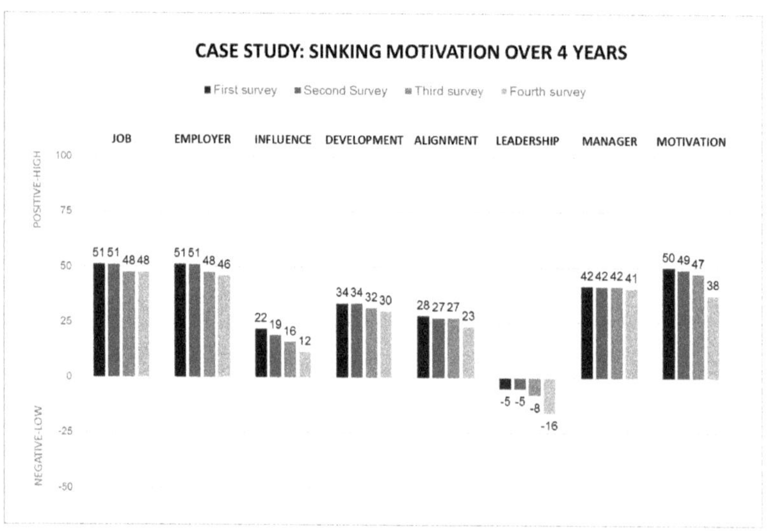

In addition to measuring motivation and drivers, we simultaneously investigated in some depth the corporate culture and internal dynamics. The data from that research was mirroring what we saw in the motivation drivers. This was a company and culture in decline.

The difficulty was that the results fell within industry benchmark standards. They commenced the four years at a relatively high level which lulled the leadership team and CEO into believing that as long as the scores were ok according to the benchmarks, then that would be good enough.

Our knowledge gleaned from employee focus groups was that the company was operating on the basis of loyalty and enthusiasm that was a hangover from the past. It was bound up with employees' sense of team camaraderie and being part of a family. Employees had a background of dedication to their work and providing service to the public. They were proud of their role and importance to the community. They were motivated in their work *despite* the company's practices and leadership. This, we warned, could not continue.

And sadly the survey results of their motivation and driver results reflects their slow decline.

Performance on all seven drivers stays steady and then, with the exception of Manager, declines over the four years. The cumulative impact so evident in the Fourth survey was a dramatic and even disastrous decline in employee motivation. In line with the loss of employee motivation, there was a loss of safety standards, performance and profit. Needless to say, as consultants we were disheartened by what we witnessed and very sad for the loyal and dedicated employees we'd met whilst conducting our research.

In the next section, I'll take a closer look at the features, nature and dynamics of each of the seven drivers. However, it's worth re-stating that all the drivers incorporate the integrated concepts of freedom within supportive systems or structure, consistent with Edward Deci's concept of "autonomy supporting controls". The potent individual driver items have been grouped to form seven driver groups (referred to as Drivers), which are labelled Job, Employer, Influence, Development, Alignment, Leadership and Manager.

Each Driver brings together the relevant features that combine or reflect some aspect of freedom within structure (or Deci's autonomy supporting controls). I did not construct this combination of features out of my imagination or from speculation; I used the evidence of factor or cluster analysis of the various survey results. Deci confirmed his speculations about the conditions promoting employee motivation using personal and laboratory observations and experience. My similar speculations have been confirmed by what is known as quantitative data, namely of the application of scientific analysis of survey results from many thousands of employees.

Seven employee motivation drivers

Figure: The seven drivers of employee motivation

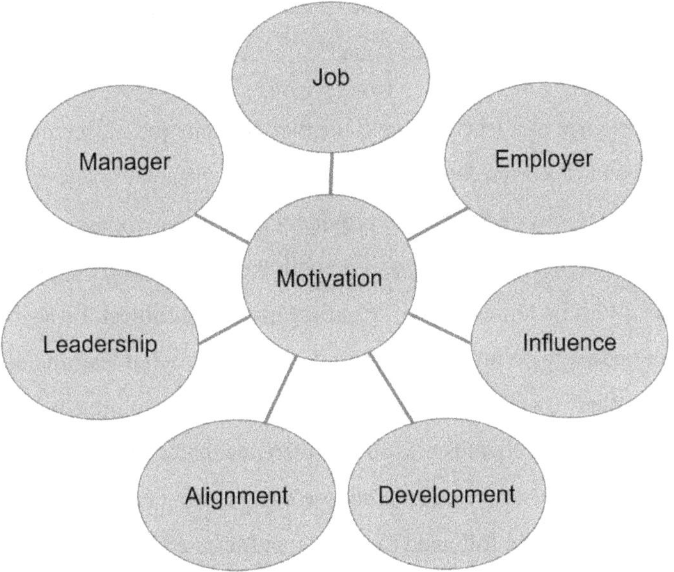

1. Job Driver

Job Driver is usually the strongest of the motivation drivers, which is not surprising when we remember what a job means to an individual. Children are invariably asked: "What do you want to do when you grow up?" A job is a defining factor in many people's lives and holds a strong place in our imaginations. Most of us bring to the job a pre-existing preference or ambition. When people do not have some idea of the type of job or role they'd prefer, they will often see this as a problematic gap in their thinking. They may say “I wish I knew what I wanted to do”, or “I don’t know what I want to do”.

With this in mind, organisations should take care to try and match their job specifications and advertisements to existing desires and ambitions of people in the community. However, even a desired job can be in reality de-motivating if some basic design and treatment elements are not followed, and indeed vice versa.

My experience as a teacher taught me that the same job, differently defined and in a different context, can generate different levels of motivation. I was once asked to provide the pre-leaving class (containing relatively low achievers) with their curriculum on ancient history. With no knowledge of or experience in the subject, I was given wide freedom to do my best. I devised a way of “teacher learning along with the class”, which consisted of sharing the subject outline with students enjoying equal access to the reference materials. Each week I invited a member of the class to choose and prepare one topic for weekly presentation followed by a class-and-teacher discussion. We were in this together!

The process, student enthusiasm, investment of time and effort was extraordinarily successful. As a result, all students passed their external exams with flying colours: an outcome that had certainly not been expected for these previously mediocre level students. The results were so far from the norm that they were audited by external examiners to confirm their correctness.

That was a year for me of real excitement and high motivation in which I too was willing to spend evenings and weekends preparing and studying to keep up with and guide the class. By contrast, some periods of being a teacher with a more rigid curriculum and less room to maneuver had left me as bored as my students. It is therefore not surprising that my research has identified one's job as the primary driver of employee motivation.

The type of job we have is very important. I remember vividly all the jobs I've ever held as they form the basic tapestry of my working life. Selecting a job is like becoming engaged, and staying in a job is like a marriage. However, there is a similar catch. Reviewing the results from client companies, I've noticed that employee motivation is invariably higher in the first year of employment – the honeymoon year. After this, motivation will drop off unless the employee is able to move up, out to new roles or on to new challenges.

I well remember one particular job in a financial services organisation. I was hired to be a human resources manager and was happy using new skills and gaining new colleagues within the objectives of the organisation. After about 18 months, I chose to attend an IT conference where we were introduced to the emerging trend of fully automated HR data systems as more efficient and economic than the outdated manual systems. I became very interested in this new technology, a technology that is common place today but was then, in 1989, a brave new world.

On returning from the conference, I rushed in to my boss to offer to undertake a feasibility study into the potential for automated HR systems for the company. My boss was a pleasant enough fellow but of his era, not overly bright, somewhat sexist and interested in his own career via managing up rather than managing down. His response was to remind me of the specifications of my role and that such a project rightly belonged to another colleague, to whom it was promptly given. Needless to say, my colleague was not at all interested and let the project lapse. My own high interest and investment in my job shriveled and eventually I started to seek employment elsewhere.

From this experience I learned that any job must allow sufficient freedom for the employee to be creative, innovative and individualistic in line with their needs. No one else wanted my project and the rationale to give it to an unwilling colleague on the basis of seniority did not serve anyone well, least of all the employer. Perhaps this was an opportunity to offer a team project or at least to let me begin an investigation. Once stopped in my tracks, it was no wonder that I found my job boring and I became apathetic, lazy, irritated, frustrated and sufficiently alienated to leave.

Obviously an organisation cannot let employees rush about in all directions but it amazes me when the new technology companies boast about encouraging innovation and creativity via games, play facilities and gyms that are external to the actual job. It is the *job itself* that needs to be motivating. Stimulation of creativity often requires nothing more than attendance at a conference, discussion with, or presentation to colleagues to get the imagination and ideas going. The main point is to not put false barriers in the way of employee input, innovation and creativity. And to remember that after about one to two years an employee needs to be stretched beyond their current activities. Simple promotion cannot always be the answer as there is less room as one goes up the ladder.

An offer of promotion wouldn't have prevented my own de-motivating experience. All I needed was permission to follow my ideas, along with some structure or objectives to support the interests of the business. Once an employee has been in their role for one or two years, they have sufficient knowledge of the organisation and its objectives to redefine or modify their role in partnership with their manager to become more useful and more valuable.

Perhaps the most important aspect of the Job driver is the fact that the employee takes up their role with a pre-existing desire to do the job and a clear idea of what they want to achieve out of it. Some organisations are realising that they can simply give employees a platform and a safe environment in which to define and develop their jobs. As long as employee activities are consistent with the business model, aim and culture of the organisation, this freedom to help define their own jobs engenders creativity, innovation, ideas and energies that generate business success.

Making Job motivating

The elements or features that combine to make a job motivating are, according to my research:

- stimulating or energizing work
- activities that make full use of the employee's skills and abilities
- a recognition that the job is intrinsically valuable and worthwhile
- one which offers variety and colour
- access to flexibility and real work life balance.

These qualities may not seem to be possible for many jobs and we often make judgements based on our own job preferences and experiences. A CEO of a multinational corporation may claim to enjoy the qualities listed above for his or her job, but doubts if there are many other jobs so blest. However, when talking with people in many different jobs it becomes clear that many of us enjoy high levels of stimulation, challenge for our skills, intrinsic value, variety and flexibility. Most people are proud and motivated by their job.

In his book 'Why we Work', the professor of psychology Barry Schwartz (2015) provides many illustrations of the motivating value of all different many types of jobs, whether lowly paid or seemingly unimportant to the outsider. He offers 'that pretty much every job has the potential to offer people satisfying work' just so long as the individual is permitted to influence the design and emphasis of the activities. If you force motivated teachers to comply with excessive performance tests, then their motivation will diminish. Leave them to exercise their unique interests and skills and they along with their students will flourish.

Thus it is with all jobs. Individuals, if asked, can help the employer or manager to ensure that their job remains motivating. Job modification in the early years may not be necessary because the job most likely offers challenges and excitement of the new and the unknown. But as years progress, motivation can wane unless allowances are made for changing employee experience, needs and growth. Thus it may be important to extend the job with a new project, a learning program or allow more work life flexibility.

However, employees' needs can change to the point where they will need to seek a new job altogether. It is a wise manager who sits down in career development discussions to predict that an employee's changing needs will not be met in the future by their current role. By predicting the employee future job needs and their evolving learning and development, the organisation might offer internal opportunities or, at the very least, manage the inevitable separation in good order.

2. Employer Driver

In a sense, the Employer driver is similar to the Job driver in that it is initiated by employees themselves. Their needs are reflected in the choice that they make in seeking or accepting employment in a specific industry or organisation. A teacher seeks a school or educational institution. An accountant seeks a finance organisation. An ecologist seeks an environmentally focused firm. Even where the individual does not have any vocational qualifications, they usually have a clear idea of the organisation that they wish to join if possible. To make sure that the Employer driver is operating to maintain or generate employee motivation, it must know what it represents not merely to its customers (an abiding obsession of companies today), but also to its employees.

I once worked with a cohort of new agents taking up positions with a policing and protection agency. Each new applicant was put through an exhaustive selection process and then, in their first year, a comprehensive and expensive training period. Despite their best efforts, the protection agency was very often losing their new intake before the end of the second year. Each resignation meant the loss of an investment of at least $300,000, which amounted to millions per year. What to do?

I ran some focus groups of new agents to investigate what was going wrong. Upon joining the organisation the majority of new agents held an extremely favourable and idealised image of their employer as an incorruptible, strong, and professional agency primarily operating to 'fight crime and win'. However, once employed they found the culture to be very strong in camaraderie and teamwork with a good dose of community interaction and the requirement to perform many detailed and laborious investigative tasks. There was a disconnect for some new agents between their expectations and the job's reality.

The agency leadership and marketing had primarily focused on their purpose to fight crime and win, and failed to promote or emphasise the collegiate teamwork and community service aspects. When the agency changed their recruitment promotions to better fit the cultural reality, their retention of new agents improved because they were now attracting people who wanted both the crime fighting purpose but also to be part of a collegiate, team based and service focused culture.

I suppose the lesson here is that an employer must check what it does and be true to itself. I can imagine how difficult it is for bank employees to remain with an organisation caught out in fraudulent practices. Once, when I asked my bank manager about a news article identifying the bank's unethical practices, she looked away in embarrassment. Like her, I once worked for an organisation which was cooking the books and using student monies for personal spending: and I chose to leave.

For small companies, making image match reality is easier and swifter to fix.

Making Employer motivating

The elements or features that combine to make the Employer motivating, according to my research, are:

- that it would be recommended to friends or family
- it demonstrates concern for one's personal or professional needs
- generates a sense of pride in the employer
- offers collaboration and good team work
- provides a positive environment with good people

Where the Job driver focused on the specifics of the role, the Employer driver focuses on the individual's role and positioning within the wider organisational framework. In this way, Employer can be understood as an extension of the Job driver.

A manager or team leader should endeavor to support collaboration and teamwork, provide an optimistic mood and offer concern for the individual. However, where an organisation culture demonstrates values that contradict those held by the individual employee (e.g. a perception that others in the business are dishonest, greedy or lack integrity) then the challenge goes beyond the team leader and rests with the organisation's senior leadership to better manage the business ethical systems, culture and values.

3. Influence Driver

We now move into the drivers that have a profound impact on employee motivation and are not burdened with failing to live up to employee's prior expectations, but that are under the full control of the manager or team leader. I remember a friend who owned a furniture factory that was once very successful, but which died a natural death as Australia began to import from developing countries where labour was cheaper. Stressed by this new challenge, he complained that his employees were not working hard enough. He commented that he thought the solution was to separate the people on the assembly line so that they could not talk.

You'll have guessed it: such a solution would have made things worse. It would have taken the fun out of the day for my friend's workers, and more importantly suppressed their interaction and shown total disrespect for them as individuals.

During the early 1980s there was enthusiasm for implementing semi-autonomous work teams. This followed the success of the innovative practices introduced by Pehr Gyllenhammar at Volvo in Sweden in the late 1970s. He abandoned the assembly line and formed workers into teams to construct a whole car; thus providing greater task variety, satisfaction and collaboration. As a result, a number of companies sought my help to restructure their workforce into semi-autonomous teams to achieve better integration between functions, such as between sales and delivery.

The most vivid experience I recall was with a coal-mining outfit that needed its miners to work in teams with their maintenance crews. So mixed teams of miners and maintenance engineers were formed for me to train into semi-autonomous work groups.

When working with one of the newly formed teams, my first task was to demonstrate how such a team might work, as no one had seen one in action. So I constructed what was grandly known as an 'experiential workshop' – in fact, just a game. The full team was divided into two sub teams of perhaps 4–5 members each. One sub team was designated as a managed group with a "manager, communications officer and the remainder as workers". The other sub team was designated semi-autonomous and left to sort itself out and to organise itself.

The teams were each given a child's dinosaur skeleton-making kit (for ages 6–8 years – so not too difficult) with the objective to complete it against two performance criteria: time and quality. Here both teams are given the same structure and boundaries. But then the teams were treated differently. The printed instructions and boxed parts were given to the manager in the managed team. He had to allocate tasks in linear order to each worker, supported by the communications officer – in other words the traditional managed-team process. The semi-autonomous team sat together, were given their printed instructions and box and simply told “go for it”.

You’ll have guessed it again: the semi-autonomous team sorted themselves out, making suggestions, exchanging information, allocating leadership roles to clever members, enjoying jokes and laughter and finishing first with a perfect model dinosaur. The managed team finished last, made a mess of the model, blamed each other – especially the manager – for the failure, disliked each other at the end and didn’t have any fun. Let me assure you that before they started, the managed team had been very confident of winning. The managed team ended up so badly that the ‘manager’ and one ‘worker’ finished their argument outside the training room with their fists!

However, many times I have played the game with teams, the semi-autonomous group, with its element of freedom, always ended up completing their model more quickly, and more happily. I was always amazed because when I first devised the exercise, I had not been sure of the outcome. Anyone can try it. Groups that are controlled, directed and over managed do not perform as well as groups where all members have their input and influence. This is why Influence is a key motivation trigger.

Making Influence motivating

The characteristics or features which combine to make the Influence driver motivating, according to my research are:

- genuine respect and dignity offered to each individual
- work that whilst it can be hard is pleasurable (even fun)
- encouragement of people to have opinions, comments or questions

- a clarity of roles, objectives and plan
- no excessive pressure or overwork falling to any one individual.

The important factor here is the level of employee participation and input that is encouraged in the relationships and the allocation of work load and planning. All too often these activities are conducted by the leadership with the outcomes handed to the employee. But the Influence driver draws us a picture of mutuality and respect for opinions contributing to the management of planning and work and the avoidance of confusion.

The employee needs to feel that he or she can have a real influence and make a contribution. This does not mean that all employee ideas are acted upon, but rather that employees are treated and respected as partners in the planning process. A suggestion box is no substitute for real influence.

4. Development Driver

As a teacher and teacher trainer, I am particularly interested in the issue of employee development and training. As you may remember from the early parts of my journey, my initial foray into understanding motivation was via student boredom, and later a thesis on student motivation and motivational drivers in school. Being essentially a teacher is one of the many reasons that I am not a spectacular manager. I perhaps have too much concern for giving support and mentoring rather than providing direction and planning.

From my perspective, the countries that are the most admirable and ultimately the most successful are those that deliver universal, quality education for all their citizens. An outstanding example is Finland: a leader in PISA (Programme for International Student Assessment) results. I also admire those organisations that are prepared to invest in the development and training of their people. But as I reviewed the research results of our many, many projects in preparation for this book, I became startled by how few leaders and managers really care about employee development and education.

I measured the amount of training (whether technical or personal) provided by each organisation in all of our research projects, on a range starting at zero days per annum and running up to 16 or more days. Again and again, results show that about 50% of all employees received 0–4 training days a year, whilst those at the most senior levels (often less than 10% of employees) were provided with the most generous training allowances in terms of days per year.

At one manufacturing company, 100% of 'low-level' employees (many of whom had left school early) had received no training at all in the year before the survey. For the next level up, it was 0–5 training days. Combined this covered 70% of all employees in the company – and those with the greatest educational needs!

One might expect something better in a government department employing over 6,000 people many of whom were highly qualified science and technology professionals. But no. A client fitting this profile had over 75% of its employees receiving less than 5 days of training and education a year, and over 25% given no training at all. By contrast about 300 of their most senior staff claimed to have received more than 16 days. Unfortunately, this story repeats itself again and again in many of our client companies from business and government.

It's easy to see why this happens. The senior levels have access to the allocation of budgets and quite happily send themselves or their immediate colleagues off to educational opportunities. And many organisations place a higher value on their more qualified and senior staff and so offer them training and development accordingly. Witness the extraordinary investment by some companies into leadership mentoring programs and even the provision of expensive overseas tertiary qualifications – benefits that indeed many of the senior executives may well be able to afford for themselves. The less senior level employees remain neglected, ignored and undervalued.

So what education, courses or training should be universally available to all employees? By definition, it *must* be more than simply the provision of technical training necessary to a job's changing requirements. Let me share with you a story about the importance of educating and developing all employees, for which I go back to my training stint with miners and engineers in the coal fields of northern NSW.

Imagine if you will a desolate Australian landscape in mid-summer, in the middle of nowhere, with nothing on the horizon except a dirty big mine and a forlorn farmhouse left over from the previous land owners and preserved as the company training facility. As you can imagine, working with this group of 12 burly men (no women in those days) in t-shirts and boots day after day meant that, after an initial period of difficulty, we all lost our awkwardness towards one another. All that is except one particular troublemaker, who I'll call Bill, who swore and was very aggressive. At one stage I asked the group to complete a small survey on their motivation, but Bill was so disruptive that I had to ask him to go outside.

Later I met Bill on the veranda to discuss what was going wrong. He reluctantly explained that he was illiterate. Had I been cleverer or more experienced, I might have guessed. Bill confessed that he'd somehow slipped through the cracks at school, but now wanted to read and had been too ashamed to seek help. The solution was simple. I organised for the company to pay and provide paid time off for Bill to attend one-on-one reading lessons. It was startling to witness the transformation in a very short time. Bill became a courteous and cooperative member of the workshop group and treated me with respect and kindness. It was charming one day when he related how he now reads with his children who help him with words they already know. I well remember how his face lit up with a smile as he recalled his new regular "playtime" with his children.

This simple diagnostic of an educational need and its remediation was of immeasurable value to Bill's workmates, his supervisor and to the mining company. Having people – whether a small or large population – in your workplace and indeed under your control surely means taking up the responsibilities of their development. Development not only raises motivation but brings with it growth and cooperation and reveals hidden employee potential. Surely each manager has the responsibility to grow their team and to ensure that each individual moves up the ladder of skills and knowledge so that they can take up more life opportunities and are more fitted to a changing capitalist and industrial landscape.

Making Development motivating

The characteristics or features which combine to make the Development driver motivating, according to my research, are:

- opportunities to learn and develop new skills
- being happy with your career prospects
- being recognised for your achievements and contributions
- a fair and non-discriminatory environment
- equality of access to training and development opportunities

The issue of training opportunities has been well covered above. It seems that higher seniority employees usually receive not only better levels of pay but also better educational treatment. All too often training is a reward handed out for the manager's friends! The keys are to plan what training is required and ensure there is appropriate curriculum development and communication. Second, tracking and recording actual hours and days spent in training for each individual and ensuring equality of access: not just for technical skills training but also for personal and professional development.

Providing equity and fairness may prove a challenge for managers in any organisation that is currently excluding or under-provisioning all of its lower level employees.

5. Alignment Driver

The Alignment driver is valued by team leaders not only for its high impact on employee motivation but also because it appears to speak to the hope of all leaders – that their people are aligned with (literally forming a straight line behind) their objectives. I've often heard leaders express a desire that all their people might operate "on the same page", or are "moving in the same direction". This brings to mind the image of a flock of birds swooping and diving as one across the sky, or a shoal of fish darting and exploding together to avoid a predator. It always makes a beautiful and breathtaking picture. Do leaders think that they can achieve such unity of purpose or movement in an organisation of people? Even with a small team, combining to keep everyone on the same path is not always guaranteed. The Alignment driver not only defines conditions that support employee motivation but also lets us into the secret as to how to get our "ducks in a row".

Beyond delivering employee and culture research client organisations, I had the opportunity to observe other activities and programs. One national postal service employing more than 7000 employees was facing the challenge of major change (are we surprised?) to convert from a bureaucratic government public agency into a commercially orientated, semi-private service and sales venture. Having defined their new direction, business objectives and structure, the leaders of the human resources function developed and implemented a very expensive (over $1 million) communication program to bring everyone into line and facing the same way. The program was very elaborate and designed to make actual physical contact with all employees via the agency of a large, highly enthusiastic volunteer team of communicators. The program involved a swift roll-out agenda of large and small presentations, multi-media messages, posters, flyers, newsletters and I know not what else. One of the observable outcomes of the communication team's many, many meetings was that they were having a lot of fun. And this masked the outcome for the remaining employees.

Analysis of survey results conducted at regular intervals we were able to compare total company results against those of the communications department.

In terms of knowledge of their strategic role and their alignment, the score for all employees combined had risen by only 6 points. For the communication department it had risen by 11 points. The motivation score for employees had risen by 1 point whilst the communication department motivation levels were up by a staggering 40 points.

This confirmed that alignment is not the outcome of good messaging. Like other drivers of motivation, alignment is a condition in which freedom is balanced by structure and input is balanced by direction. The communication department team were profoundly experiencing the positive elements of the Alignment driver. The rest of the employees were just being told about the direction they were expected to take.

Making Alignment motivating

The characteristics or features which combine to make the Alignment driver motivating, according to my research, are:

- encouragement to be innovative and independent in thinking
- being allowed to contribute to work processes and planning
- empowerment to make relevant role decisions
- encouragement to use your initiative and experience
- having clear knowledge of organisation's direction and your role in it

The Alignment driver is one of the purist examples of the most effective way to promote employee motivation. However, very few managers would list its features as high on their list of responsibilities. It is important that managers check how well they are encouraging employee independence, decision-making and input. Managers may find it easy to communicate the organisation direction passed down from leadership but fail in balancing within their team its objectives, plans, processes with the opportunity or freedom to contribute.

6. Leadership Driver

I was once talking to a very experienced business leader who had been a CEO himself and had extensive interactions with other leading CEOs as Chairman of a senior executive mentoring club. He maintained that the main contributor to company success was the leader. And indeed, looking at the salary packages of corporate leaders today, you'd have to say his attitude is shared by many boards of management.

The interesting thing about the Leadership Driver is that when I first started out in organisational research in the early 1980s, it didn't exist. Maybe because leaders were at that time so distant from their people? Whatever the reason, it was a fact that leaders were not on the radar as correlating with, or significantly impacting on, employee motivation. However, by the year 2000, leaders had increased their impact on employees' motivation and now figured as a significant driver.

My experience with CEOs is somewhat limited, despite having worked with so many companies. However, one leader has remained as a standout memory. This was a large scientific and professional organisation with highly qualified staff from top to bottom. Their results demonstrated that Leadership scored the lowest when compared with other drivers, and specifically around the issue of two-way communication between leaders and the organisation.

So many leaders go into denial when faced with criticism. However, this CEO immediately took up the challenge. In front of his people at the workshop presentation of the survey results he spoke up, "I offer an open invitation to anyone who wishes to join me on Friday late afternoons for a coffee and chat. I will hold this on the outside deck next to my office. This is for anyone between 4 and 6pm, whether junior or senior. You can ask me questions, make comments or just chat." This offer became the strategy known as "David's Deck" and was highly successful in the eyes of the employees, and also in raising the Leadership driver score the next year.

I noted that some of the most successful leaders were, like David, extraordinarily courteous and treated all staff with respect and dignity. So they're not all bad, and stuck in the 19th century, Taylor scientific management ethos. However, the power accorded a CEO is extraordinary and can corrupt even the most admirable of individuals.

Of course, it's even more dangerous when a CEO doesn't have an admirable stature or superior skills. I once witnessed the operation of a dysfunctional leadership team – a destructive dynamic created and sustained by the CEO. The organisation was a utilities concerned with delivering an essential public service. Of its 3500 employees, 58% were frontline technicians and engineers who constituted the key delivery cohort and on which rested the business's reputation with customers, government and the wider public. The leader of this Delivery division was far and away the best qualified and most effective leader. Not surprisingly, the organisation's highest employee motivation scores came from his Delivery division.

However, for reasons never apparent to me, this delivery division executive was demeaned, ignored and criticized in executive team meetings. His projects were blocked and his needs were unsupported. There were obvious tensions in the meetings and most of the key decisions were made by the CEO and selected colleagues later, in "the corridors". The shabby treatment of the delivery executive and his division was confirmed to me by many other executives. More significantly, comments in focus groups made it plain that this dysfunction and disunity was well known to the wider group of employees down the line. Inevitably this state of affairs had a negative impact on motivation and performance of the entire organisation which eventually led to wider community and political repercussions.

Making Leadership motivating

The characteristics or features which combine to make Leadership motivating, according to my research, are:

- leadership teamwork

- being seen to be strong, effective and dynamic
- no barriers to communication with employees (open door policy)
- setting the example of honesty and integrity
- being the primary source of timely information

The point here is that our research demonstrated that it's not just the leader but the coherence and unity of the executive team that has the greatest impact on employee motivation. The Leadership driver promotes employee motivation by means of the behaviours and attitudes of the leadership team. Motivation is the outcome of the leadership team's capacity to demonstrate unity and cooperation, strength and effectiveness and to lead by example in terms of honesty and integrity.

The other elements in this driver suggest the need for close communication and dialogue between the leadership team and employees, who do not then need to rely on rumour and scuttlebutt for information about what's going on in the organisation. So it's not just the CEO or individual leader: a coherent, strongly united and openly communicating leadership *team* is the key to the Leadership driver.

7. Manager Driver

For many management authorities and in many books written about management, the manager or team leader is writ large. For example, Robert Sutton (*Good Boss, Bad Boss*, 2010) maintains that managers always overestimate their social and intellectual skills and need constant self-awareness for a reality check on their performance. Good management is a little like good teaching. You and I might choose a course at a university on the quality of the lecturer over the nature of the topic. Similarly, many employees will seek to join or stay with a good manager.

But perhaps being a so-called *good manager* is not that easy, in the same way being a good parent is not that easy. Having control over and responsibility for other people reveals all that is good or bad about a personality. Some people have a talent for being a manager: I for one don't have it. I'm by nature a teacher, and I am a good one. When I've been a manager, I tend to revert to the skills of teaching, which don't really work when managing. There are many types of people who are a long way from being a manager. The local general practitioner, veterinarian, geriatric caregiver and priest don't spring to mind as good managers.

There are also many people that I call "accidental managers". They are good at their job, they have high technical skills, are leaders in their fields and suddenly find themselves managing a group of people as a reflection of their expanding sphere of influence and activity. The teacher who becomes head of a department, the owner of an expanding small business, the statistician who inherits a research unit – they're all people who never thought to manage and in fact who prefer not to. Managers by accident!

So you who are good, bad or indifferent managers, you'll be relieved to know that whilst you do influence employee motivation, you have the *least* impact of the seven drivers.

Making Manager motivating

The characteristics or features which combine to make Leadership motivating, according to my research, are:

- being open and easy to talk to
- good communicator providing needed information
- effective and good basic management skills
- developing and bringing out the best in members of the team
- assisting with coaching, training and performance

The scores on the elements of the manager driver are invariably high. We appear to have in Australia a superior cohort of managers who know their job and lead their people well. There are many books and courses that help to remind managers of their need to be open and good communicators, organisers, and performance coaches for team members.

However, a bad manager is a disaster for the team. Where a manager is fond of the exercise of power rather than being a mentor to a cooperative team, then personality faults can become enhanced. Bad temper, slow decision making, rudeness, playing favourites, capricious actions and irrational decisions means a frightening and demoralizing work environment.

Case study: Team differences

Most people in business assume that smaller companies have an easier time when it comes to managing their handful of small teams when compared with large organisations which manage large multipurpose teams. It is said that a small business can more easily provide a consistently positive and similar experience regarding leadership, management and general employment conditions. This case study shows how wrong that assumption can be. Whether the organisation is small or large, there can be major differences between teams, between their levels of motivation and their response to the working environment.

The first chart below is from a company with more than 4,000 employees organized into eight divisions working across three locations within the same city and state. The senior leadership team comprised ten individuals, eight of whom led a division.

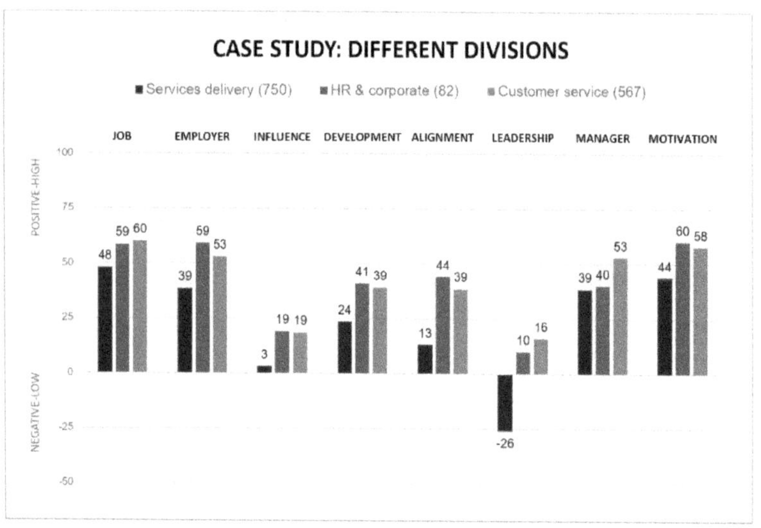

Survey results from three divisions - delivery, customer service and corporate - illustrate significant internal differences apparent at division level. The diversity of the results may be explained by company size and the difficulties associated with delivering consistency of practice and culture across such large groups.

So if we turn to a smaller business we might expect to see results that are more consistent. The second chart is from a technology small to medium size (SME) employing 30 people working together in one office with their CEO beside them. The business prides itself on an open, collegiate and fun culture. It also provides an abundance of modern employment ideas and conditions such as flexible hours, bring your dog to work days, social clubs and leading edge technology tools for people to use. It is a high energy, vibrant and apparently happy workplace. Given how integrated all the teams appeared to be, it was expected that team results would show similar motivational needs and priorities.

Survey results from the two most critical functions – sales and service – whilst at the higher end of scores, were a surprise because the results were so dramatically different.

The sales team of ten were highly motivated by strong performance on nearly all seven drivers. Whilst the customer service team of 12 people had much lower motivation levels from weaker scores particularly on the Leadership, Development and Influence drivers.

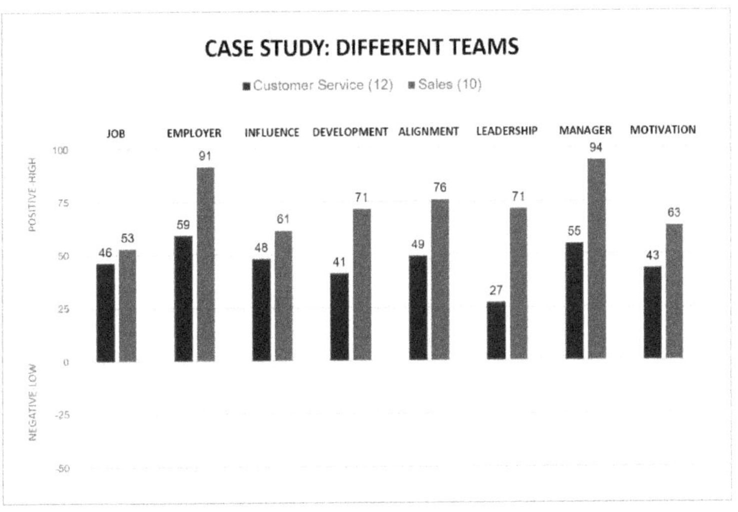

By seeing these results alone, you might never conclude that these teams worked side by side, with the same manager, and same opportunities and culture. This information was a real surprise to the CEO who was the Leader for both teams and thought that he had provided equality in terms of Development and Influence for all his employees. The 'noisier' sales team were clearly getting more attention than the customer service team whose needs for input and to hear more from their leader were not being met.

The CEO said of these results, "I can see that I've been neglecting the service team to their detriment; yet the service team is so critical for the business."

The lesson from these studies is that teams and divisions, like people are all different and important motivational differences in teams operate in small businesses as well as in large businesses.

Motivation management replaces scientific management

Stanford University professor Jeffrey Pfeffer reviewed numerous studies across many industries in *The Human Equation* (1998) and found that workplaces that offer employees work in a way that is engaging, motivating, meaningful and included some autonomy are more profitable than workplaces that treat employees like cogs. He cites many studies of companies that are more sustainable and have higher sales if they use enlightened employee practices, respecting and valuing their people.

In a recent and celebrated book (*Why We Work*, 2015), the American psychologist Barry Schwartz provides numerous interviews with menial task workers who confirm that they work for fulfilment, meaning, purpose and satisfaction. He quotes a group of lowly custodians in a public hospital who enjoyed caring for, joking with and calming down patients – despite the fact that their official duties make no mention of "patients" and they received no pay for this extra work. In fact, Schwartz confirms Edward Deci's research that external motivators of money, rewards and performance indicators often undermine employee intrinsic motivation.

Despite repeated anecdotal and scientific support for encouraging employee motivation since Maslow first introduced the idea, business is not always listening. Many large organisations continue to prefer the inheritance of Frederick Taylor and his scientific management with discrete tasks, measurement and pay for performance. As Alan Wooldridge, Schumpter columnist for *The Economist* pointed out in September 2015, powerful companies such as Google and Motorola are adopting digital Taylorism with more sophisticated technological performance-measurement tools, including the innovation of "sociometric" badges.

Figure: Tripartite Motivation Model showing organisational drivers and outcomes

WORKPLACE DRIVERS

MOTIVATION NEEDS

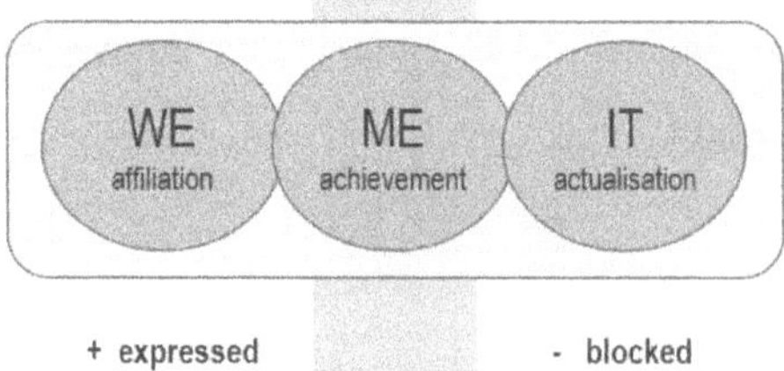

+ expressed - blocked

BEHAVIOUR & ATTITUDES

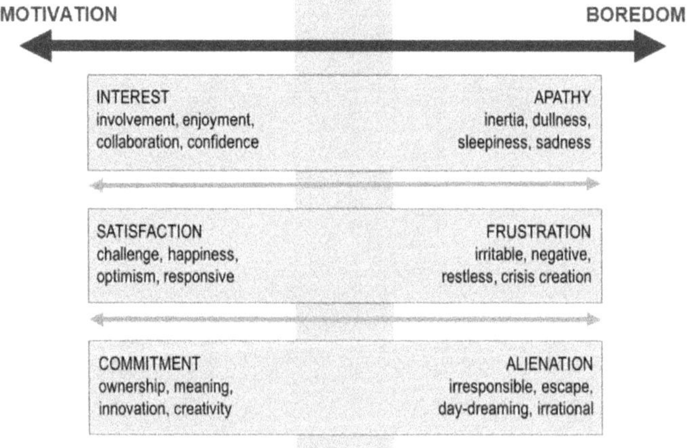

ORGANISATIONAL OUTCOMES

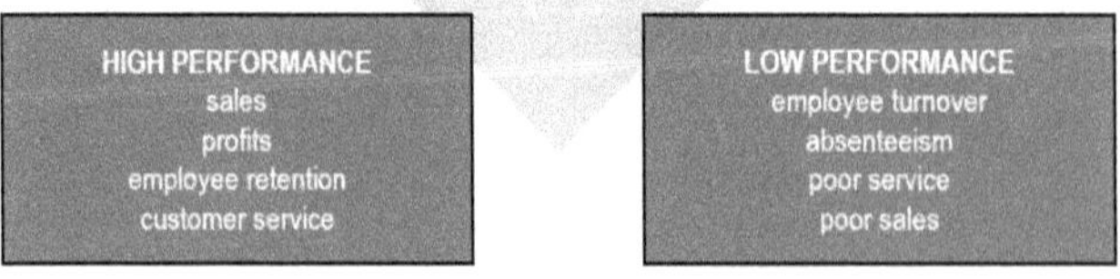

HIGH PERFORMANCE
sales
profits
employee retention
customer service
LOW PERFORMANCE
employee turnover
absenteeism
poor service
poor sales

These are being applied not only to front-line workers but also to managers and specialists, and offering very high performance bonuses as sweeteners. Wooldridge notes that stopwatch management and pay for performance continues to conquer new territories, such as Amazon's "rank or yank" policy.

Rose Powell of the *Australian Financial Review* (2015) has described the toxic culture of the big tech companies. She cites the *New York Times*' August 2015 investigation into Amazon, which all but confirmed the notion that digital disruption is the domain of ruthless leaders who foster unrelenting expectations and slaughter their staff's spirits in a monthly bloodbath, also known as KPI (key performance indicator) reviews.

Many, especially larger, organisations continue to introduce or maintain these counterproductive practices – despite the mountain of evidence that chunking knowledge undermines creativity, measurement robs jobs of their pleasure, pushing people beyond their limits institutionalises "burn and churn", and peer reviews encourage backstabbing.

I listened to Barry Schwartz being interviewed on Radio National Australia (December 2015) and he was asked the question: "Why, when there is proof that supporting motivation is a better way than command and control in the workplace, do managers ignore the evidence?" His answer was that the importance and effectiveness of employee intrinsic motivation was always being revived over the ages but seemed to get as quickly forgotten. "My book simply revives what has been known for a long time – but its message may well disappear again. I hope not," he said. Alternatively, he suggested that managers just liked being the boss and using the old directive command and control ways.

My answer would have been rather different. Motivating employees takes effort, time, patience and emotional intelligence. And even then you can fail. It is similar to bringing up a family with both love and support: trying to provide children with the right balance between freedom to grow, to express and to develop, modified by rules, guidance and order. Using a social metaphor, balancing freedom of the press with the rule of law. Human relations are messy and often difficult and to get them right invariably requires humility, insight and wisdom. These traits are not readily found in leaders and managers. Well, they may be found, but they're not sufficiently valued or supported. To take these motivating practices into the workplace requires a passionate belief that this will deliver the best outcomes for both the individuals and the success of the business.

Power conferred by money, politics or importance tends to forget the humanity that lies beneath and can create distance between leaders and employees. That is why smaller organisations are less likely to forget the need for supporting intrinsic motivation. When numbers become large the individual becomes dispensable – whether at war or work. Organisations, regardless of size, that respect the humanity of their employees, provide sufficient autonomy and latitude, opportunity to speak up and participate whilst at the same time putting in place appropriate objectives, planning and training, will benefit and are more likely to succeed over the long term.

However, whether the organisation is large or small, supporting or releasing intrinsic employee motivation requires a balancing act for the manager to deliver autonomy within structure. That is why the drivers described in this chapter may provide the reader with real benefit. They offer a framework to help us achieve the autonomy with structure balance. Irrespective of one's ability with people, the seven drivers provide a road map that's clear and simple.

I've met managers who lack people skills and so are nervous and shy of interaction. Having people skills certainly helps in getting the best out of your team. But understanding the seven most potent drivers of employee motivation will assist managers to inject the right balance of freedom with freedom-supporting structure. They may help to make poor people managers good, and good people managers better.

CHAPTER 8: YOUR MOTIVATION

The complexity of motivation

IF WIKIPEDIA IS ANY GUIDE, interest in the topic of motivation has increased dramatically over recent years. Unfortunately, the result is rather a muddle or confusion between myriad different theories and approaches. But for me and I hope by now for readers, it is quite simple. Motivation is an intrinsic, innate and natural feature of living things. It is the arousal of energy or movement emanating from needs or instincts towards the attainment of an object or aim. According to the *Macquarie Dictionary*, motivation suggests a strong reason or need that drives someone to do something.

My research, outlined in some detail in this book, has identified three innate instincts or needs in humans. Two reflect our animal nature of procreation and survival. The third is uniquely human in the need to attain some sort of spiritual, creative, intellectual or higher, often non-material, objective. We might call it the human spirit or the need to be human. The evidence for this third need is our capacity to dream, to use our imagination and to picture things in the past and the future, or even beyond the immediate tangible physical world.

To position the three needs in our everyday life, I have given them descriptive names of Affiliation, Achievement and Actualisation – or if you prefer, the catchier labels of We, Me and It.

The problem with understanding or describing motivation is that it is expressed in so many ways. It is accompanied by myriad feelings, behaviours and outcomes. Motivation means so many pathways and so many objectives that it presents an overwhelming picture of complexity. Every activity and attainment of humanity finds its origins in the three needs or instincts, not nicely separated but interlocked and interwoven. Sometimes one need seems to dominate. For example, a politician's career ending urgent need to be with their family (affiliation), or a mother's overwhelming desire to return to work to be something 'more than just a mother' (achievement). At different times one motivational may be more urgent than another. Depending on the circumstances, time of day, individual character, personality, education and experiences, it is possible to have any one of the three needs dominant. The other two do not disappear or cease operation, they just move a little to the background.

For this reason, the strength of one of our three needs may alter in relation to the other needs. Imagine a symphony where all instruments are present and playing but from time to time, the string instruments are louder than the wind instruments. Thus I may score higher on one aspect of motivation today than I will a week from today. Today at home my Affiliation need may score higher than the Achievement need. Another time at work my Actualisation need may be stronger than both the Affiliation and Achievement needs.

Within this chapter is a short "My Motivation" self-assessment to help you discover your own level of need in terms of Affiliation, Achievement and Actualisation. If you think of your current employment when answering the questions, then the lowest score will provide you with an insight into what is most lacking at your work, which need is the least met. For example, if your Achievement need is the lowest, the issue at work for you is likely to be insufficient individuality, promotion, use of your skills and talent, opportunity to 'win' or input. Use the discussion in the rest of this chapter to gain insights into what promotes or suppresses your energy. Find out how to increase and maintain motivation in your own life or alternatively how to fix too little motivation in your job or primary work activity.

Despite the fact that it is possible for one need to be more fully expressed or stronger than another, this does not change the fact that all three needs will be operating. More often than not, our actions are a result of the three needs being synthesised and compounded. My need in writing this book is surely a combination of the Affiliation need to join the community of writers, the Achievement need to write a book and the Actualisation need to create something lasting, unique or original.

In considering motivation, it is difficult to separate the need from its objective, the outcome from its cause. So at the outset I took a different and new path through this difficulty, namely the study of boredom.

How did we get here?

This section is primarily for readers who are starting this book with this final chapter. If you have read through the book from the beginning, you may like to skip ahead to the motivation self-assessment.

Just as medicine finds the path to health by pinpointing the sickness and just as psychoanalysis finds the path to personal freedom by pinpointing the underlying blockage, so our path to understanding motivation has begun with a closer look at boredom. It recalls one of the most famous of Arthur Conan Doyle's detective stories, "Silver Blaze" (1892) where Sherlock Holmes points out that the key to the mystery is "the curious incident of the dog in the night time". The policeman Gregory says: "But the dog did nothing in the night time." Holmes replies "*That* is the curious incident." Boredom is the curious incident of motivation not happening.

From the stories in this book, it becomes clear that our own personal experience provides the swiftest pathway to understanding boredom. Then we can look to others to confirm the generality of our own experience. Finally, we can look to research and the statistically analysed experience of many people to confirm the universality of the original personal experience. This staged path from personal insight, through external examples to generalised confirmation is known in scientific terminology as the process from observation to hypothesis to theory.

My personal journey offers a picture of this process. I first observed that if I could not speak up or disagree in a lecture, then I became bored. This experience was replicated and generalised in the literature setting out statements of school students who complain of boredom because they have to be silent. From this I was able to hypothesise or claim that lack of verbal expression caused boredom. This claim was then confirmed as a theory by my surveys of thousands of employees. That they were not able to ask questions, disagree or comment correlated with increasing boredom and decreasing motivation. I'd discovered a universal truth by the study of an insight that began with a personal experience. The recognition and conviction that boredom and silence are linked began with understanding of the self. For this reason, I am ending this book with a focus not on other people (and their role as student or employee or whatever) but on you, the reader. This section is not a "how to" section but a "let me understand me" section.

Needs expressed or suppressed

So let's begin with another look at the link between boredom and motivation. The significant nature of needs-based motivation is that it is either expressed or suppressed. It will not go away by being ignored, at least not for long. In Australian society, our most severe form of punishment is prison where individuals are not free to leave or to express themselves. They are restricted and confined – even more so in solitary confinement. We use prison as a punishment because it prevents the expression of our needs for affiliation, achievement and actualisation. For imprisoned people, the non-expression of our motivational needs or instincts can be a very great source of unhappiness or even pain. Whilst most of us are not in actual prison, we can be in situations that feel like it, such as a dreary job or a bad marriage.

Thinking back to my university experience of not commenting due to the external situation of a lecture hall, suppression did not end there. In fact, I was not physically prevented from speaking but chose, albeit unconsciously, to restrain myself on the basis of timidity or courtesy. In this way we can further impose the suppression of our motivation by conniving with the situation or authorities to place additional internal prohibitions on expression. Here we are talking of self-censorship and self-inhibition: think of the overly good child who is expected to sit still and then never learns to play freely.

John's story

John was of my students when I taught English at a boys-only secondary high school. This was a low performing class and students were not expected to achieve university entrance. John performed very well in classroom interaction but distressingly never performed well enough to receive a pass mark on his essays. One night I decided read one of his essays out aloud to try and see what was going wrong. I made a startling discovery. John wrote almost perfect sentences but always with one or two words missed or transposed. Instead of writing "Byron is one of the better known romantic poets" he would write "Byron is of the poets known romantic better". A tired teacher marking essays after hours, as I was, would just skim over these sentences and give a fail mark to the essay. Having found the problem, I was able to trace the faulty transpositions of words. Reorganised correctly, the result was a very good essay.

I had a private chat with John, showed him the problem and explained how he had mangled otherwise perfect sentences. The question now was not what went wrong but why. In our conversation, John explained that he was not allowed to say anything at home: his opinion was forbidden at the dining table. I realised that his obedience to his father to never express an opinion had extended to his school essays.

John provides an example of an individual imposing further controls on their behaviour or attitude to follow an external authority figure. John had built upon an externally imposed suppression of his need to express himself with a further internally imposed suppression. This is known as internalising the authority figure, or in Freudian terms, internalisation of the 'super ego'. John's father may not have meant to undermine his son's scholastic achievements but that was the outcome.

The story has a happy ending. Once he discovered that he was spoiling his own sentences and had recognised that he need not obey his father in school, John's performance improved dramatically. He came top of the English class, was moved into higher grades and ultimately went to university and became a lawyer. I learned of his success many years later when we ran into each other in a grocery store.

Human motivation is a permanent source of energy that can be expressed or suppressed, and expression is better for our health and happiness. However, in today's more permissive and liberal society, there are as many problems arising from the untamed expression of energies as from excessive parental controls. Not all prohibitions are bad. Education, civilisation and social morality have an important part to play in ensuring that our expression of energies and motivation are civilised.

Whilst a cliché, it is nonetheless true that human energies can be used to both create and destroy. This is why it's important for individuals to develop as many skills and abilities as possible to ensure that they have creative as opposed to destructive outlets for their energies. Sport, crafts, art, exercise, work, cooking, building, writing, singing, organisation or whatever activity you can lay your hands provide freedom and permission combined with a holding security and structure. Freedom without controls is permissiveness and can lead to destructive behaviours and outcomes. Freedom to express our needs can only occur where there are what Edward Deci calls "autonomy promoting controls". We need all the skills, abilities and education available combined with freedom and opportunity to be able to exercise and express our own motivation and to be able to support it in others.

Jason's story

Jason Day is a champion Australian golfer – at the time of writing ranked world number 1. His story is a remarkable one. After the death of his golf-playing father when he was 12 years of age, Jason became troubled and played truant, joining gangs and getting drunk. He vacillated between apathy, anger and escaping from school.

Obviously bored and unable to utilise his energies, he was fortunate to have a mother who made tremendous sacrifices to send Jason to a boarding school that offered golf as part of the curriculum. Here Jason was provided with the stability and opportunity to continue to play golf. He says that his first encounter with the school's golf professional (who remains his caddy today) ended in a fight! Nevertheless, he went on to excel at golf, suffering many years of near misses in the championship rounds but finally winning the trifecta of three majors in 2015. Jason Day is now 27 and is said to have "a sweet swing, a cool demeanor and tireless work ethic." His success continues to this day where his achievements go from strength to strength.

Boredom is the default setting for many individuals, especially those with high energy needs such as teenagers, who do not have the right conditions of structure combined with freedom, of trained skills combined with autonomy.

The greatest playwright of all time, William Shakespeare, in *Hamlet* (Act 1 Scene 2) describes boredom. Hamlet has just lost his father, witnessed his uncle take the throne, seen his mother marry his uncle in haste, suspects foul play and, in the final words of the soliloquy, identifies his problem: “But break, my heart, for I must hold my tongue!”

This suppression results in the best description of boredom I’ve yet found.

> *“O! that this too, too solid flesh would melt,*
> *Thaw and resolve itself into a dew;*
> *Or that the Everlasting had not fix’d*
> *His canon ‘gainst self-slaughter! O God! God!*
> *How weary, stale, flat, and unprofitable,*
> *Seem to me all the uses of this world.”*

Your motivation self-assessment

If you are highly motivated today this quiz may be hard to answer. So you may like to wait until you are less motivated or think about the last time you were bored and remember what that felt like.

To get to the interpretation that reflects your current motivational profile, you need to work through the following three steps.

1. Thinking about your current circumstances, select four of the following statements that are most applicable or truest for you today.

I am feeling a bit isolated and sad.	A
I am feeling a bit fed up, frustrated and even angry.	B
I don't feel like I'm achieving anything.	B
I don't feel connected or that I belong.	A
Time drags and I feel like what I'm doing will never end.	C
I can't express myself easily or as much as I'd like to.	C
I am finding it harder and harder to get out of bed in the morning.	B
I just don't care anymore about what I'm doing.	A
I don't believe it what I'm doing. It has no meaning for me.	C

2. Look at the letters beside your chosen statements. Which letter appears most often beside your chosen four statements? Mostly A's, B's or C's?

3. Use the results to select your current personal motivational need

   Mostly A's read section **A: need for Affiliation (We)**
   Mostly B's read section **B: need for Achievement (Me)**
   Mostly C's read section **C: need for Actualisation (It)**

A: need for Affiliation (We)

When our need for friendship, family, colleagues and community interaction is being ignored or unexpressed, we experience a range of negative emotions and behaviours. These allow us to recognise that our problem is the blocking or negating of the Affiliation instinct – the 'We'.

Probably the most frequent symptoms of Affiliation boredom are loneliness, sadness and a sense of isolation. Other less obvious symptoms include emotional eating, sleepiness, apathy, inertia, a sense of dullness, and a sense of servitude, a sense of sameness, lack of interest, laziness and the very slow passage of time. The world seems a cold, bleak and friendless place.

If your score on the test shows low Affiliation, then your 'We' need is not being sufficiently met. This may be because you fall into the 30% of the population that has a stronger Affiliation need than others, or because the situation (your job, marriage or whatever you decided would be the focus of your test) lacks the conditions to meet this particular instinct or need.

The answer is to look for, or to create, opportunities for interaction and play with others. Join a club, organise a party, participate in a team, spend more time with your family, invest more time and effort in friends.

The Affiliation need is the most obvious need to many people who are lucky enough to live in relative security and safety. The need to have a family and to nurture that family is very powerful. However, the need for affiliation can extend to others who are not our family. We have colleagues at work, friends from school and university, fellow members in clubs or groups, neighbours and associates in our community and even interactions with strangers in the street or public places. We do not need to conform to the current definition of "having the nuclear family" to satisfy the affiliate need. It is all about nurturing, caring for and supporting our fellow human beings in whatever circumstances. In fact, where people care for nature and the environment as part of the "family of all living things" they are possibly expressing in large part their Affiliate drive. Let me illustrate with a true story.

A Buddhist monk has an orphanage at the foot of the Himalaya. The area is incredibly beautiful with a vista of green valleys and blue sky. The local population is scattered and poverty stricken with tiny huts to live in and not much food. The monk cares for many children in his orphanage who are the victims of poverty or loss of parents. He tells the children the story of a baby boy thrown away by a desperate mother and found by chance by his grandmother who brings the boy up. "And who is that?" he asks the children. "It's you." they chorus with delight.

At the orphanage there is a traumatized girl who has real behavioural difficulties with fighting and bed-wetting. But with quiet, unfailingly good-tempered care, she becomes well and in turn acts as an older sister to the next new child who arrives at the orphanage. The monks have four or five such helpers and in considering a new applicant, they protest that they have no room because children are already sleeping two to a bed. But they long to help all who ask.

The monk has this to say about his orphanage: "As a child myself, I missed out on childhood. But with these children, I am able to enjoy eighty-five childhoods."

Today, there's much media commentary that business people, especially males, do not give enough time to family or friends. This conscious refocusing on the demands of the Affiliate need occurs because it happens to be the weakest when compared with the other needs. Remember the origin of the Affiliate need is the instinct for procreation, which gives way in the face of the instinct for survival. Even rats stop reproducing when they have to fight for their survival.

B: need for Achievement (Me)

When our need or instinct for Achievement – or for 'Me' – is not being met, the most frequent symptoms are frustration, depression, irritability, rigidity, aggression, negativity, pessimism, restlessness, bad temper and unprovoked anger. The world is a hostile and unforgiving place and there appears to be insufficient recognition of your contributions and value.

If your score on the test is lowest for Achievement, it may be because your situation does not allow you to excel or to shine or it may be that you are part of the 30% of people in the world that has a stronger Achievement need than others.

The answer is to join or initiate projects that will allow you to make best use of your talents and ideas. Achievement is the one need that can be expressed equally with either language or action. Freedom of speech is the essential quality of a democracy and as Freud said, "Speech is practice action." This may be why we admire writers, poets, playwrights and journalists – because they are able to express dangerous and aggressive ideas in the written or spoken word where they are rendered harmless, useful and constructive.

The Achievement need is the one we celebrate and notice the most. The fight between politicians holds a fascination as we observe both winners and losers. The Olympic Games celebrates physical prowess and pits individual against individual, and team against team. "Citius – Altius – Fortius" (faster – higher – stronger) are the words first expressed by a Dominican priest in 1891 at a youth sports event and then adopted as the motto of the Olympic movement. This represents the athletic, technical, moral and educational aspirations that symbolise the Achievement need.

Are we a little suspicious, even fearful of the Achievement or 'Me' need because it is all about aggression, winning and indeed hints of war? There is a relatively recent policy in childcare where "everyone gets a prize". Instead of allowing one child to be the acknowledged the single winner, the Achievement need is subverted by parents into the caring and sharing Affiliation need, where everyone gets a reward. However, we should not forget that the Achievement need generates the wealth of nations. Business and mercantilism is all about beating the competition, winning the dominant position, protecting against takeovers, and grabbing the lion's share of the market. Whilst we would not like the world to be exclusively dominated by the Achievement need, it provided the human urgency and energy to bring about such phenomena as the industrial and digital revolutions, the exploration of our planet and indeed our forays into space.

The problem with less enlightened societies is that they allow the strongest and loudest to dominate the rewards. The prize goes to the toughest. And women with their child-bearing role are seen as keepers of the Affiliation need, and men by their fighting role are keepers of the Achievement need. Why are men most likely to beat up their partners, claim the higher wages, grab the most powerful roles? Because they can. It's surely time for a civilised and educated society to recognise that the three needs are shared equally between the sexes.

Where your Achievement score is lowest in terms of your employment or central activity, then it is time to seek new challenges and to extend your area of interest. It may mean moving jobs but more often it means seeking a new role, offering a new project, talking with the boss to upgrade your position, or seeking extra skills or education outside by taking up courses and joining training institutions. Many people change their career or profession halfway through their working lives. What suited the young adult may not fully utilise the talents, attitudes and experiences of the mature adult. But whatever the new choice, it must satisfy the need for survival, achievement and individuality – the 'Me' need!

C: need for Actualisation (It)

We experience Actualisation boredom when the need for meaning, purpose or something more important is blocked or suppressed.

The most frequent symptoms of Actualisation boredom are irresponsibility, escapism (in terms of alcohol, drugs, or more usefully travel and physical removal), loss of concentration, daydreaming, mental absenteeism or even hallucinations. The extreme symptoms are not often experienced, as the individual will quickly remove themselves from such an unpleasant range of sensations and behaviours by mental escape or physical escape of running away or leaving the job.

In 1945, the celebrated and brilliant Georges Simenon wrote a 'Maigret' novel called *Monsieur Monde Vanishes*, in which a seemingly happy, married professional man simply walks out one day to vanish into thin air – surely a picture of escape from Actualisation boredom.

If your score on the test is lowest on Actualisation, then your 'It' need is not being sufficiently expressed. This may be because you fall into the approximately 30% of the population that has a stronger actualisation need than others, or because your situation simply gives this need little or insufficient outlet or recognition.

The answer is to indulge in a few moments of self-analysis to imagine what you would do or be if there were no family or financial impediments. There is a problem with the Actualisation – or 'It' – need in that we use the language of higher or special attainment to explain it. I talk of the creative instinct, the spiritual instinct, the need for meaning and purpose. But the Actualisation need is not an esoteric urge belonging exclusively to the more superior or creative of our fellow human beings. It is the essence of our humanity and is therefore a central "mover and shaker" in all of us.

Certainly it's easy to recognise the creative urge in an artist, or the higher calling of those brave souls who provide help and sustenance to refugees in war zones. But all people have a central core of humanity that needs to be expressed. It may not be as obvious but it's there. In Australia, 32% of the population – some 6.1 million people – participate in formal volunteering. If asked, volunteers respond that their primary reason is to make a difference, to contribute in a meaningful way. It always amuses me when politicians boast that they entered politics to "make a difference" as if their contribution is somehow unique and rare. Each and every one of us has the need to make a difference, to achieve something higher, to create beauty or to embrace a spiritual path. It may not always seem impressive to outsiders, but as long as it has meaning for you, then it is an expression of the Actualisation need.

Actualisation and play

I have made reference to two very useful books in helping to understand the operation of needs-based intrinsic motivation in us. In *Why we do what we do* (1995), Edward Deci quotes research on life aspirations and comments that "people who are healthiest focus on developing satisfying personal relationships, growing as individuals and contributing to the community" - surely the We, Me and It of tripartite motivation.

Those who marched against the Vietnam War, who invest their time in saving the planet, who serve in a soup kitchen, who arrange flowers to beautify the home, who join a choir, who go to church, who set up a social network group to promote democracy; they are all motivated by something great or bigger in the human spirit. In *Why We Work* (2015), Barry Schwartz suggests that people who see work as a calling (rather than just a career) find it the most satisfying, vital to their identity and making the world a better place. But I would go further. I contend that it's not in work but in play that the expression of the 'It' need (commitment, identity, meaning and making a difference) is most often found. Everyone regards some part of their life (whether specifically called work, play or something else) as a calling and contributing to making the world a better place. For each and every one of us is imbued with some level of Actualisation motivation. If motivation is operating at all in a free individual, then the It element will be alive and well. Putting it another way, we all, whether great or small, seek love, work and play.

There was a time in the last century when mathematics was not considered a suitable topic for women to study as their brains were considered not adequate to the task. In fact, at the time so-called scientific proof of the brain differences were developed and published. We now know that that was not science, but merely wishful thinking on the part of the dominant male society. In the same way, there are some people today that consider a higher calling is only for the special few – the top scientists, creative artists or spiritual leaders. This is patently not true. All men and all women have the human instinct for creativity and spirituality. This may not always be visible to the outsider but is available as a source of inspiration and purpose throughout our lives. It's not a matter of not having the Actualisation wishes or instinct as suggested by the poet Thomas Gray:

> *"Far from the madding crowd's ignoble strife*
> *Their sober wishes never learnt to stray"*
> (Elegy written in a country churchyard).

We all have the same wishes, needs and desires that "stray" to seek purpose and meaning, irrespective of our birth, status and education.

I know a young and very smart lawyer who I'll call Susan. She earns good money in her day job. But at the weekends she devotes at least one day to pro bono work for victims of rape and abuse. I asked her about this. She replied: "I do it for fun. I know that sounds strange when you consider the suffering of my clients. But what I mean is that it doesn't feel like work. It's my choice. I get a real high having made a difference to a woman's life. I would miss it if I stopped."

I met a cleaner, Jane, who offered a similar opinion about her work. "I used to work for four people but now I have just two who I have chosen to keep on," she told me. "I can do much more with their homes and make them beautiful. Before it was just cleaning. But now it doesn't feel like work as I can set higher standards and make a difference. When I walk out I feel really proud."

Whilst the working world can be dominated by money and competition, the world of play deals in images, dreams, imagination, pictures, drama, gods, heroes and make believe. Surely it this play aspect of who we are that provides the materials that feed or answer our need for Actualisation.

Where the Actualisation score is lowest in terms of the work or activity that you have chosen to measure against, then it's time to seek greater personal choice and playfulness. Many jobs provide a level of imaginative, pleasurable or creative opportunities. But if the job is too much like a prison for your soul and your true nature, it's time to seek fun or to indulge in the activities that you have always loved, perhaps even as a child. I once saw a documentary about a farm in the Dales in England, where a mother and son sold their herd of milking cows and replaced them with pigs and sheepdogs. They swapped work they hadn't enjoyed for activities they loved – rearing and training sheepdogs. They still worked just as hard as they had with the herd of milking cows, but they had swapped "hard work" for "play" as an expression of actualisation: the 'It' motivation.

Motivation, education and the world of work

There continues to be an ideological battle between those who adhere to a humanist approach (like myself) or a Taylorist approach to the organisation of the workplace. Frederick Winslow Taylor (1856-1995) held in his model of scientific management that workers are basically lazy or self-interested and will only respond to rewards and punishments. This requires that work be broken down into performance-measurable chunks – the assembly line.

This adherence endures despite the research evidence that you and I work better, more efficiently and more creatively if our intrinsic motivations are given the appropriate direction, freedom and support in the completion of a whole not part task.

The fight between the two approaches is I think a matter of trust. Either I trust others to achieve what I need them to achieve or I do not. If I trust them then I'll provide sufficient autonomy within structure. If I don't trust them, then I'll control the way in which people will be allocated the work broken down into mini tasks, with each performance measured.

Both Deci and Schwartz hold that the Taylorist approach to the workplace has a negative impact on the way people and society behaves. Give workers performance-managed tasks and they will become the lazy, rather stupid people described by Taylor (based, I might add, on his observations of the uneducated lower classes of the United States in the late 19th and early 20th centuries).

But Deci and Schwartz have missed an important consideration. Whilst humans may well respond to their Taylorist workplace by becoming de-motivated and lazy, they are much more influenced by their early years of education: "My school made me!" This is exactly why education has changed from a tradition of learning by rote to learning through investigation, questioning, projects and the support of youthful creativity. Our social school-based values of egalitarianism, physical freedom, the importance of play and the wonder of independence have combined to generate a generation of intrinsically motivated adults. This has been a miracle of innovation heralding the digital revolution and also advances in science, the arts and social awareness.

As a result, many of us refuse to be bound by the irrational and stultifying controls exercised over our work and professional skills by the manager or the boss. In my relatively short working career (excluding the period in education), I've been sacked by a manager who was stealing student funds, sent on a nine-hour journey to collect a vanity publication, denied promotion for seeking to use my initiative, and had my intellectual property stolen. So, despite the loss of earning power and of security, I – like many others – started my own company and put in place the planning needed to keep my freedom on track.

Sadly, in Australia, my teaching friends tell me that the business world and its lack of trust in intrinsic motivation is already beginning to invade the world of education. Is there a creeping belief that children are inherently lazy and self-interested? They tell me that teachers are now having curriculum subjects broken down into mini tasks against which the student's (and by extension the teacher's) performance is measured. This will inevitably flow on to the way the children are educated and handled. We should resist this invasion by the business world and remember that trust begins in childhood. The over-controlling manager is simply a product of our society. The Taylorist workplace was a product of the previous system of education. The flowering of an intrinsically motivated society and workplace where each member can express all three needs of Affiliation, Achievement and Actualisation is a product of the best in our modern education. We should remember this.

We have a choice.

ILLUSTRATIONS

The majority of the artwork images in this book are included courtesy of the National Gallery of Art, Washington DC, United States of America.

https://images.nga.gov/en/page/show_home_page.html

Introduction	Artist: Eugène Delacroix Title: Young Tiger Playing with its Mother (Jeune tigre jouant avec sa mère), Dated 1831
Chapter 1	Artist: Mary Cassatt Title: Little Girl in a Blue Armchair, Dated: 1878
Chapter 2	Artist: George Caleb Bingham Title: The jolly flatboatmen, Dated: 1846
Chapter 3	Artist: George Catlin Title: Oneida Chief, His Sister, and a Missionary, Dated: c.1861
Chapter 4	Artist: Mary Cassatt Title: Children Playing on the Beach, Dated: 1884

Chapter 5	Artist: Auguste Renoir Title: Claude Monet, Dated: 1872
Chapter 6	Artist: Unknown Title: The Acrobats, Dated: 1825 (or after)
Chapter 7	Artist: Charles-François Daubigny Title: Le Marais aux canards (Swamp with Ducks), Dated: 1862 Courtesy of Yale University Art Gallery
Chapter 8	Artist: Jean-Baptiste-Camille Corot Title: The Artist's Studio, Dated: c.1868

REFERENCES

Alderfer, C.P., (1972) *The ERG theory of motivation (existence, relatedness, growth)* Administrative Science Quarterly 489-505

Ambrose M.L. and Kulik, C. T. (1999) *Old Friends, New Faces: Motivation Research in the 1990s.* Journal of Management June 25: 231-292,

Blishen, E. (1958) *The School That I'd Like* London Pelican

Beck, R.C. (1978) *Motivation:Theories and Principles.* New Jersey. Prentice Hall

Bergler, E. (1945) *On the disease-entity boredom (alyosis) and its Psychopathology.* Psychiatric Quarterly 19, 38-51

Bettelheim, B. (1967) *The Empty Fortress.* NY Macmillan

Bexton,W.H., Heron, W., & Scott, T.H. (1954) *Effects of Decreased Variation in the Sensory Environment.* Canadian Journal of Psychology 8, 2, 70-76

Bolles, R.C. (1967) *Theory of Motivation.* NY Harper and Row

Bong, M. (1996) *Problems in Academic Motivation Research: advantages and disadvantages of their solutions.* Contemporary Educational Psychology 21. 149-165

Brook, D (2011) *It's not about you* New York Times

Burgess, P (2003) *The Development of the Intrinsic Drives System.* Linkup International

Burton, D.L. (1962) *Trailing Clouds of Boredom Do They Come.* The English Journal 51, 259-265

Carr, S. (2016) *Motivation, Educational Policy and Achievement.* A critical perspective. Routledge.

Conan Doyle, A. (1892) *The Memoirs of Sherlock Holmes* PanMcMillan

Cofer, C.N. and Appley, M.H. (1964) *Motivation: Theory and Research.* NY, John Wiley

Daniel, T. and Metcalf,G. (2005) *The Science of Motivation* Virginia SHRM

De Cecco, J.P (1968) *The Psychology of Learning and Instruction* New Jersey Prentice-Hall

Deci. E. L. (1975) *Intrinsic Motivation* New York Plenum

Deci, E.L. (1995) *Why we do what we do.* Penguin,

Deci, E.L. & Ryan, R. (2002). *Handbook of Self-Determination Research.* NY Rochester Press,

Drury, A. (1982) *Individual differences in boredom proneness and task effectiveness at work.* Personnel Psychology 35, 141-151

Fenichel, O. (1951) *On the Psychology of Boredom* Collected Papers New York, David Lewis

Fogelman, K. (1976) *Bored Children* New Society 37, 15

Fowler, S. (2014) *What Maslow's Hierarchy Won't Tell You About Motivation.* Harvard Business Review. Nov.

Fisher C.D. (1993) *Boredom at Work: a neglected concept* Discussion Paper 19 Bond University

Freud, S (1923) *The Ego and the Id.* Complete Works 19 13-48 London Hogarth Press

Freud, S (1925) *Negation* Complete Works 19, 235 London Hogarth Press

Freud. S (1933) *New Introductory Lectures on Psychoanalysis* Complete Works 22 London Hogarth Press

Friedan, B. (1963) *The Feminine Mystique*. Norton,

Green, Joshua (2014) *Moral Tribes: Emotion, reason and the gap between us and them.* Penguin

Greenson, R.R. (1953) *On Boredom* Journal of the American Psycho-analytic Association. 1,7-21

Haidt, Jonathan. (2012) *The Righteous Mind: why good people are divided by politics and religion.* Pantheon

Hall, J.F. (1961) *Psychology of Motivation.* NY Lippencott

Herzberg, F., (1966) *Work and the Nature of Man* Cleveland World

Herzberg F. (1983) *Motivation.* Cleveland World

Hill, A.B. and Perkins, R.E. (1985) *Towards a model of boredom.* British Journal of Psychology 76, 235-240

Hinds, J-M. (1993) *Employee boredom in the workplace*. PhD Thesis. Macquarie Graduate School of Management.

Hinds, J-M. (1994) Employee *boredom in the workplace: a contribution to motivational theory and organisational productivity*. New Directions in Management. Sydney McGraw-Hill.

Hinds, J-M. (1995) The *Hinds Model of Company Success.* Sydney Millenium Press.

Hofstede, G (1980) *Motivation, Leadership and Organisation.* Organisational Dynamics 9. 42-63

Kallio, P. (1964) *Boredom and Fatigue in School Children.* Educational Research 6, 235-8

Kanter, R. M. (2001). *Evolve! Succeeding in the digital culture of tomorrow*. Harvard Business Press

Korman, A.K. (1974) *The Psychology of Motivation.* New Jersey, Prentice Hall

Kuhn, R. (1976) *The Demon of Noontide: Ennui in Western Literature* New Jersey. Princeton

Kular. S et al (2008) *Employee Engagement – A Literature Review* Kingston University

Latham, G. P. and Pinder, C. (2005) *Work Motivation Theory and Research at the Dawn of the Twenty-First Century.* Annual Review of Psychology Vol. 56: 485-516

Lawrence, P.R & Nohria, N., (2002) *Driven: how our human nature shapes our choices*. San Francisco Jossey-Bass

Leckart, B. and Weinberger, L.G. (1980) *Up from Boredom, Down from Fear.* NY. Richard Marek.

Lewin, Kurt (1947) *Frontiers in Group Dynamics: concept, method and reality in social science.* Human Relations 1.36.

MacLeod, D & Clarke, N. (2009) *Engaging for Success: enhancing performance through employee engagement* Report to the UK Government,

Mael, F and Jex, S (2015) *Workplace Boredom: an integrative model.* Group Organisation Management. 40. 2. 131-159

McClelland, D.C. (1953) *The Achievement Motive* NY Appleton-Century-Crofts

McNeill, D. and Freiberger, P. (1993) *Fuzzy Logic.* Melbourne Bookman Press

Mann, S. & Cadman, R. (2014) *Does being bored make us more creative?* Creativity Research Journal, Volume 26, Issue 2.

Maslow, A. H. (1943) (1954?) *Motivation and Personality* New York Harper and Row

Nohria, N, Groysberg, B. and Lee, L (2008) *Employee Motivation* Harvard Business Review 86. 78-84

Obuchowski, C.W. (1968) 1964? *Boredom the unhidden enemy* French Review 37

Pink, D. (2009) *Drive: The Surprising Truth About What Motivates Us.* Canongate

Pfeffer, J. (1998) *The Human Equation: building profits by putting people first.* Harvard Business School Press

Powell,R. (2015) *Toxic company cultures are easy in tech. Here's how the new wave is building something better* in the Australian Financial Review newspaper.

Schaufeli, W.B & Salanova, M. (2014) *Burnout, Boredom and Engagement in the Workplace*; Chapter 12: An Introduction to Contemporary Work Psychology. Wiley & Sons.

Schwartz B. (2015) *Why We Work* Ted Books

Skinner B.F. (1974) *About Behaviourism* Mass Market Paperbacks

Smith, R.P. (1981) *Boredom: a review.* Human Factors 23. 3. 329-340

Smith. S. (1963) *Clinical Aspects of Perceptual Isolation* Royal Society of Medicine 55. 1003

Spacks, P.M. (1995) *Boredom: The literary history of a state of mind* University of Chicago Press

Sutton, R. (2010) *Good Boss, Bad Boss: how to be the best and learn from the worst.* Business Plus.

INDEX

www.ingramcontent.com/pod-product-compliance
Lightning Source LLC
Chambersburg PA
CBHW060544210326
41519CB00014B/3341

9780994603609